Introducing MLOps
How to Scale Machine Learning in the Enterprise

Mark Treveil and the Dataiku Team

Beijing · Boston · Farnham · Sebastopol · Tokyo

Introducing MLOps

by Mark Treveil, and the Dataiku Team

Copyright © 2021 Dataiku. All rights reserved.

Published by O'Reilly Media, Inc., 1005 Gravenstein Highway North, Sebastopol, CA 95472.

O'Reilly books may be purchased for educational, business, or sales promotional use. Online editions are also available for most titles (*http://oreilly.com*). For more information, contact our corporate/institutional sales department: 800-998-9938 or *corporate@oreilly.com*.

Acquisitions Editor: Rebecca Novack
Development Editor: Angela Rufino
Production Editor: Katherine Tozer
Copyeditor: Penelope Perkins
Proofreader: Kim Wimpsett

Indexer: Ellen Troutman-Zaig
Interior Designer: David Futato
Cover Designer: Karen Montgomery
Illustrator: Kate Dullea

December 2020:   First Edition

Revision History for the First Edition

2020-11-30:   First Release

See *http://oreilly.com/catalog/errata.csp?isbn=9781492083290* for release details.

978-1-492-08329-0

[LSI]

Table of Contents

Part I.   MLOps: What and Why

Part II.   MLOps: How

Preface

We've reached a turning point in the story of machine learning where the technology has moved from the realm of theory and academics and into the "real world"—that is, businesses providing all kinds of services and products to people across the globe. While this shift is exciting, it's also challenging, as it combines the complexities of machine learning models with the complexities of the modern organization.

One difficulty, as organizations move from experimenting with machine learning to scaling it in production environments, is maintenance. How can companies go from managing just one model to managing tens, hundreds, or even thousands? This is not only where MLOps comes into play, but it's also where the aforementioned complexities, both on the technical and business sides, appear. This book will introduce readers to the challenges at hand, while also offering practical insights and solutions for developing MLOps capabilities.

Who This Book Is For

We wrote this book specifically for analytics and IT operations team managers, that is, the people directly facing the task of scaling machine learning (ML) in production. Given that MLOps is a new field, we developed this book as a guide for creating a successful MLOps environment, from the organizational to the technical challenges involved.

How This Book Is Organized

This book is divided into three parts. The first is an introduction to the topic of MLOps, diving into how (and why) it has developed as a discipline, who needs to be involved to execute MLOps successfully, and what components are required.

The second part roughly follows the machine learning model life cycle, with chapters on developing models, preparing for production, deploying to production, monitoring, and governance. These chapters cover not only general considerations, but

MLOps considerations at each stage of the life cycle, providing more detail on the topics touched on in Chapter 3.

The final part provides tangible examples of how MLOps looks in companies today, so that readers can understand the setup and implications in practice. Though the company names are fictitious, the stories are based on real-life companies' experience with MLOps and model management at scale.

Conventions Used in This Book

The following typographical conventions are used in this book:

Italic
Indicates new terms, URLs, email addresses, filenames, and file extensions.

`Constant width`
Used for program listings, as well as within paragraphs to refer to program elements such as variable or function names, databases, data types, environment variables, statements, and keywords.

`Constant width bold`
Shows commands or other text that should be typed literally by the user.

`Constant width italic`
Shows text that should be replaced with user-supplied values or by values determined by context.

O'Reilly Online Learning

For more than 40 years, *O'Reilly Media* has provided technology and business training, knowledge, and insight to help companies succeed.

Our unique network of experts and innovators share their knowledge and expertise through books, articles, and our online learning platform. O'Reilly's online learning platform gives you on-demand access to live training courses, in-depth learning paths, interactive coding environments, and a vast collection of text and video from O'Reilly and 200+ other publishers. For more information, visit *http://oreilly.com*.

How to Contact Us

Please address comments and questions concerning this book to the publisher:

O'Reilly Media, Inc.
1005 Gravenstein Highway North
Sebastopol, CA 95472
800-998-9938 (in the United States or Canada)
707-829-0515 (international or local)
707-829-0104 (fax)

We have a web page for this book, where we list errata, examples, and any additional information. You can access this page at *https://oreil.ly/intro-mlops*.

Email *bookquestions@oreilly.com* to comment or ask technical questions about this book.

For news and information about our books and courses, visit *http://oreilly.com*.

Find us on Facebook: *http://facebook.com/oreilly*

Follow us on Twitter: *http://twitter.com/oreillymedia*

Watch us on YouTube: *http://www.youtube.com/oreillymedia*

Acknowledgments

We would like to thank the entire Dataiku team for their support in developing this book, from conception to completion. It's been a true team effort and, like most things we do at Dataiku, rooted in fundamental collaboration between countless people and teams.

Thanks to those who supported our vision from the beginning of writing this book with O'Reilly. Thanks to those who stepped in to help with writing and editing. Thanks to those who provided honest feedback (even when it meant more writing and rewriting and re-rewriting). Thanks to those who were internal cheerleaders and, of course, those who helped us promote the finished product to the world.

MLOps: What and Why

CHAPTER 1

Why Now and Challenges

Machine learning operations (MLOps) is quickly becoming a critical component of successful data science project deployment in the enterprise (Figure 1-1). It's a process that helps organizations and business leaders generate long-term value and reduce risk associated with data science, machine learning, and AI initiatives. Yet it's a relatively new concept; so why has it seemingly skyrocketed into the data science lexicon overnight? This introductory chapter delves into what MLOps is at a high level, its challenges, why it has become essential to a successful data science strategy in the enterprise, and, critically, why it is coming to the forefront now.

MLOps Versus ModelOps Versus AIOps

MLOps (or ModelOps) is a relatively new discipline, emerging under these names particularly in late 2018 and 2019. The two—MLOps and ModelOps—are, at the time this book is being written, largely being used interchangeably. However, some argue that ModelOps is more general than MLOps, as it's not only about machine learning models but any kind of model (e.g., rule-based models). For the purpose of this book, we'll be specifically discussing the machine learning model life cycle and will thus use the term "MLOps."

AIOps, though sometimes confused with MLOps, is another topic entirely and refers to the process of solving operational challenges through the use of artificial intelligence (i.e., AI for DevOps). An example would be a form of predictive maintenance for network failures, alerting DevOps teams to possible problems before they arise. While important and interesting in its own right, AIOps is outside the scope of this book.

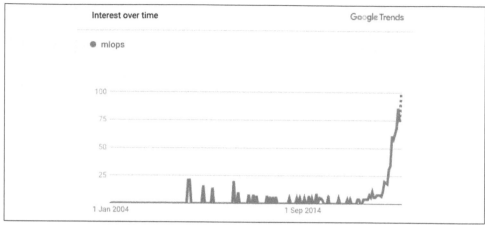

Figure 1-1. Representation of the exponential growth of MLOps (not the parallel growth of the term "ModelOps")

Defining MLOps and Its Challenges

At its core, MLOps is the standardization and streamlining of machine learning life cycle management (Figure 1-2). But taking a step back, why does the machine learning life cycle need to be streamlined? On the surface, just looking at the steps to go from business problem to a machine learning model at a very high level, it seems straightforward.

For most traditional organizations, the development of multiple machine learning models and their deployment in a production environment are relatively new. Until recently, the number of models may have been manageable at a small scale, or there was simply less interest in understanding these models and their dependencies at a company-wide level. With decision automation (that is, an increasing prevalence of decision making that happens without human intervention), models become more critical, and, in parallel, managing model risks becomes more important at the top level.

The reality of the machine learning life cycle in an enterprise setting is much more complex, in terms of needs and tooling (Figure 1-3).

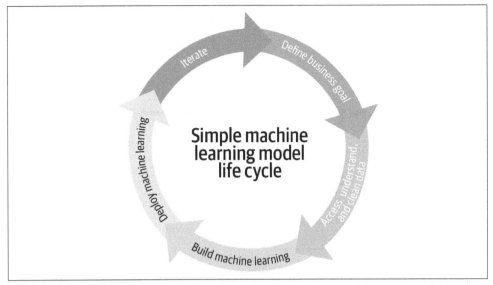

Figure 1-2. A simple representation of the machine learning model life cycle, which often underplays the need for MLOps, compared to Figure 1-3

There are three key reasons that managing machine learning life cycles at scale is challenging:

- There are many dependencies. Not only is data constantly changing, but business needs shift as well. Results need to be continually relayed back to the business to ensure that the reality of the model in production and on production data aligns with expectations and, critically, addresses the original problem or meets the original goal.

- Not everyone speaks the same language. Even though the machine learning life cycle involves people from the business, data science, and IT teams, none of these groups are using the same tools or even, in many cases, share the same fundamental skills to serve as a baseline of communication.

- Data scientists are not software engineers. Most are specialized in model building and assessment, and they are not necessarily experts in writing applications. Though this may start to shift over time as some data scientists become specialists more on the deployment or operational side, for now many data scientists find themselves having to juggle many roles, making it challenging to do any of them thoroughly. Data scientists being stretched too thin becomes especially problematic at scale with increasingly more models to manage. The complexity becomes exponential when considering the turnover of staff on data teams and, suddenly, data scientists have to manage models they did not create.

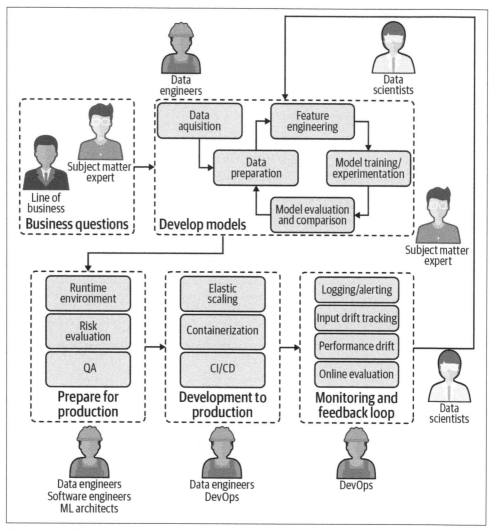

Figure 1-3. The realistic picture of a machine learning model life cycle inside an average organization today, which involves many different people with completely different skill sets and who are often using entirely different tools.

If the definition (or even the name MLOps) sounds familiar, that's because it pulls heavily from the concept of DevOps, which streamlines the practice of software changes and updates. Indeed, the two have quite a bit in common. For example, they both center around:

- Robust automation and trust between teams
- The idea of collaboration and increased communication between teams

- The end-to-end service life cycle (build, test, release)
- Prioritizing continuous delivery and high quality

Yet there is one critical difference between MLOps and DevOps that makes the latter not immediately transferable to data science teams: deploying software code into production is fundamentally different than deploying machine learning models into production. While software code is relatively static ("relatively" because many modern software-as-a-service [SaaS] companies *do* have DevOps teams that can iterate quite quickly and deploy in production multiple times per day), data is always changing, which means machine learning models are constantly learning and adapting—or not, as the case may be—to new inputs. The complexity of this environment, including the fact that machine learning models are made up of both code and data, is what makes MLOps a new and unique discipline.

What About DataOps?

To add to the complexity of MLOps versus DevOps, there is also DataOps, a term introduced in 2014 by IBM. DataOps seeks to provide business-ready data that is quickly available for use, with a large focus on data quality and metadata management. For example, if there's a sudden change in data that a model relies on, a DataOps system would alert the business team to deal more carefully with the latest insights, and the data team would be notified to investigate the change or revert a library upgrade and rebuild the related partition.

The rise of MLOps, therefore, intersects with DataOps at some level, though MLOps goes a step further and brings even more robustness through additional key features (discussed in more detail in Chapter 3).

As was the case with DevOps and later DataOps, until recently teams have been able to get by without defined and centralized processes mostly because—at an enterprise level—they weren't deploying machine learning models into production at a large enough scale. Now, the tables are turning and teams are increasingly looking for ways to formalize a multi-stage, multi-discipline, multi-phase process with a heterogeneous environment and a framework for MLOps best practices, which is no small task. Part II of this book, "MLOps: How," will provide this guidance.

MLOps to Mitigate Risk

MLOps is important to any team that has even one model in production because, depending on the model, continuous performance monitoring and adjusting is essential. By allowing safe and reliable operations, MLOps is key in mitigating the risks induced by the use of ML models. However, MLOps practices do come at a cost, so a proper cost-benefit evaluation should be performed for each use case.

Risk Assessment

When it comes to machine learning models, risks vary widely. For example, the stakes are much lower for a recommendation engine used once a month to decide which marketing offer to send a customer than for a travel site whose pricing and revenue depend on a machine learning model. Therefore, when looking at MLOps as a way to mitigate risk, an analysis should cover:

- The risk that the model is unavailable for a given period of time
- The risk that the model returns a bad prediction for a given sample
- The risk that the model accuracy or fairness decreases over time
- The risk that the skills necessary to maintain the model (i.e., data science talent) are lost

Risks are usually larger for models that are deployed widely and used outside of the organization. As shown in Figure 1-4, risk assessment is generally based on two metrics: the probability and the impact of the adverse event. Mitigation measures are generally based on the combination of the two, i.e., the model's severity. Risk assessment should be performed at the beginning of each project and reassessed periodically, as models may be used in ways that were not foreseen initially.

5 x 5 risk matrix					
Highly probable	5 Moderate	10 Major	15 Major	20 Severe	25 Severe
Probable	4 Moderate	8 Moderate	12 Major	16 Major	20 Severe
Possible	3 Minor	6 Moderate	9 Moderate	12 Major	15 Major
Unlikely	2 Minor	4 Moderate	6 Moderate	8 Moderate	10 Major
Rare	1 Minor	2 Minor	3 Minor	5 Moderate	6 Moderate
	Very low	Low	Medium	High	Very high

Probability (vertical axis) — Impact (horizontal axis)

Figure 1-4. A table that helps decision makers with quantitative risk analysis

Risk Mitigation

MLOps really tips the scales as critical for risk mitigation when a centralized team (with unique reporting of its activities, meaning that there can be multiple such teams at any given enterprise) has more than a handful of operational models. At this point, it becomes difficult to have a global view of the states of these models without the standardization that allows the appropriate mitigation measures to be taken for each of them (see "Matching Governance with Risk Level" on page 107).

Pushing machine learning models into production without MLOps infrastructure is risky for many reasons, but first and foremost because fully assessing the performance of a machine learning model can often only be done in the production environment. Why? Because prediction models are only as good as the data they are trained on, which means the training data must be a good reflection of the data encountered in the production environment. If the production environment changes, then the model performance is likely to decrease rapidly (see Chapter 5 for details).

Another major risk factor is that machine learning model performance is often very sensitive to the production environment it is running in, including the versions of software and operating systems in use. They tend not to be buggy in the classic software sense, because most weren't written by hand, but rather were machine-generated. Instead, the problem is that they are often built on a pile of open source software (e.g., libraries, like scikit-learn, Python, or Linux), and having versions of this software in production that match those that the model was verified on is critically important.

Ultimately, pushing models into production is not the final step of the machine learning life cycle—far from it. It's often just the beginning of monitoring its performance and ensuring that it behaves as expected. As more data scientists start pushing more machine learning models into production, MLOps becomes critical in mitigating the potential risks, which (depending on the model) can be devastating for the business if things go wrong. Monitoring is also essential so that the organization has a precise knowledge of how broadly each model is used.

MLOps for Responsible AI

A responsible use of machine learning (more commonly referred to as Responsible AI) covers two main dimensions:

Intentionality
> Ensuring that models are designed and behave in ways aligned with their purpose. This includes assurance that data used for AI projects comes from compliant and unbiased sources plus a collaborative approach to AI projects that ensures multiple checks and balances on potential model bias. Intentionality also

includes explainability, meaning the results of AI systems should be explainable by humans (ideally, not just the humans who created the system).

Accountability

Centrally controlling, managing, and auditing the enterprise AI effort—no shadow IT (*https://oreil.ly/2k0G2*)! Accountability is about having an overall view of which teams are using what data, how, and in which models. It also includes the need for trust that data is reliable and being collected in accordance with regulations as well as a centralized understanding of which models are used for what business processes. This is closely tied to traceability: if something goes wrong, is it easy to find where in the pipeline it happened?

These principles may seem obvious, but it's important to consider that machine learning models lack the transparency of traditional imperative code. In other words, it is much harder to understand what features are used to determine a prediction, which in turn can make it much harder to demonstrate that models comply with the necessary regulatory or internal governance requirements.

The reality is that introducing automation vis-à-vis machine learning models shifts the fundamental onus of accountability from the bottom of the hierarchy to the top. That is, decisions that were perhaps previously made by individual contributors who operated within a margin of guidelines (for example, what the price of a given product should be or whether or not a person should be accepted for a loan) are now being made by a model. The person responsible for the automated decisions of said model is likely a data team manager or even executive, and that brings the concept of Responsible AI even more to the forefront.

Given the previously discussed risks as well as these particular challenges and principles, it's easy to see the interplay between MLOps and Responsible AI. Teams must have good MLOps principles to practice Responsible AI, and Responsible AI necessitates MLOps strategies. Given the gravity of this topic, we'll come back to it multiple times throughout this book, examining how it should be addressed at each stage of the ML model life cycle.

MLOps for Scale

MLOps isn't just important because it helps mitigate the risk of machine learning models in production; it is also an essential component to massively deploying machine learning efforts (and in turn benefiting from the corresponding economies of scale). Going from one or a handful of models in production to tens, hundreds, or thousands that have a positive business impact requires MLOps discipline.

Good MLOps practices will help teams at a minimum:

- Keep track of versioning, especially with experiments in the design phase
- Understand whether retrained models are better than the previous versions (and promoting models to production that are performing better)
- Ensure (at defined periods—daily, monthly, etc.) that model performance is not degrading in production

Closing Thoughts

Key features will be discussed at length in Chapter 3, but the point here is that these are not optional practices. They are essential tasks for not only efficiently scaling data science and machine learning at the enterprise level, but also doing it in a way that doesn't put the business at risk. Teams that attempt to deploy data science without proper MLOps practices in place will face issues with model quality and continuity—or, worse, they will introduce models that have a real, negative impact on the business (e.g., a model that makes biased predictions that reflect poorly on the company).

MLOps is also, at a higher level, a critical part of transparent strategies for machine learning. Upper management and the C-suite should be able to understand as well as data scientists what machine learning models are deployed in production and what effect they're having on the business. Beyond that, they should arguably be able to drill down to understand the whole data pipeline (i.e., the steps taken to go from raw data to final output) behind those machine learning models. MLOps, as described in this book, can provide this level of transparency and accountability.

CHAPTER 2

People of MLOps

Even though machine learning models are primarily built by data scientists, it's a misconception that only data scientists can benefit from robust MLOps processes and systems. In fact, MLOps is an essential piece of enterprise AI strategy and affects everyone working on, or benefiting from, the machine learning model life cycle.

This chapter covers the roles each of these people plays in the machine learning life cycle, who they should ideally be connected and working together with under a top-notch MLOps program to achieve the best possible results from machine learning efforts, and what MLOps requirements they may have.

It's important to note that this field is constantly evolving, bringing with it many new job titles that may not be listed here and presenting new challenges (or overlaps) in MLOps responsibilities.

Before we dive into the details, let's look at the following table, which provides an overview:

Role	Role in machine learning model life cycle	MLOps requirements
Subject matter experts	• Provide business questions, goals, or KPIs around which ML models should be framed. • Continually evaluate and ensure that model performance aligns with or resolves the initial need.	• Easy way to understand deployed model performance in business terms. • Mechanism or feedback loop for flagging model results that don't align with business expectations.
Data scientists	• Build models that address the business question or needs brought by subject matter experts. • Deliver operationalizable models so that they can be properly used in the production environment and with production data. • Assess model quality (of both original and tests) in tandem with subject matter experts to ensure they answer initial business questions or needs.	• Automated model packaging and delivery for quick and easy (yet safe) deployment to production. • Ability to develop tests to determine the quality of deployed models and to make continual improvements. • Visibility into the performance of all deployed models (including side-by-side for tests) from one central location. • Ability to investigate data pipelines of each model to make quick assessments and adjustments regardless of who originally built the model.
Data engineers	• Optimize the retrieval and use of data to power ML models.	• Visibility into performance of all deployed models. • Ability to see the full details of individual data pipelines to address underlying data plumbing issues.
Software engineers	• Integrate ML models in the company's applications and systems. • Ensure that ML models work seamlessly with other non-machine-learning-based applications.	• Versioning and automatic tests. • The ability to work in parallel on the same application.
DevOps	• Conduct and build operational systems and test for security, performance, availability. • Continuous Integration/Continuous Delivery (CI/CD) pipeline management.	• Seamless integration of MLOps into the larger DevOps strategy of the enterprise. • Seamless deployment pipeline.
Model risk managers/ auditors	• Minimize overall risk to the company as a result of ML models in production. • Ensure compliance with internal and external requirements before pushing ML models to production.	• Robust, likely automated, reporting tools on all models (currently or ever in production), including data lineage.
Machine learning architects	• Ensure a scalable and flexible environment for ML model pipelines, from design to development and monitoring. • Introduce new technologies when appropriate that improve ML model performance in production.	• High-level overview of models and their resources consumed. • Ability to drill down into data pipelines to assess and adjust infrastructure needs.

Subject Matter Experts

The first profile to consider as part of MLOps efforts is the subject matter experts (SMEs); after all, the ML model life cycle starts and ends with them. While the data-oriented profiles (data scientist, engineer, architect, etc.) have expertise across many areas, they tend to lack a deep understanding of the business and the problems or questions that need to be addressed using machine learning.

Subject matter experts usually come to the table—or, at least, they *should* come to the table—with clearly defined goals, business questions, and/or key performance indicators (KPIs) that they want to achieve or address. In some cases, they might be extremely well defined (e.g., "To hit our numbers for the quarter, we need to reduce customer churn by 10%" or "We're losing $N per quarter due to unscheduled maintenance; how can we better predict downtime?"). In other cases, the goals and questions may be less well defined (e.g., "Our service staff needs to better understand our customers to upsell them" or "How can we get people to buy more widgets?").

In organizations with healthy processes, starting the machine learning model life cycle with a more defined business question isn't necessarily always an imperative, or even an ideal, scenario. Working with a less defined business goal can be a good opportunity for subject matter experts to work directly with data scientists up front to better frame the problem and brainstorm possible solutions before even beginning any data exploration or model experimentation.

Without this critical starting point from subject matter experts, other data professionals (particularly data scientists) risk starting the machine learning life cycle process trying to solve problems or provide solutions that don't serve the larger business. Ultimately, this is detrimental not only to the subject matter experts who need to partner with data scientists and other data experts to build solutions, but to data scientists themselves who might struggle to provide larger value.

Another negative outcome when SMEs are not involved in the ML life cycle is that, without real business outcomes, data teams subsequently struggle to gain traction and additional budget or support to continue advanced analytics initiatives. Ultimately, this is bad for data teams, for SMEs, and for the business as a whole.

To add more structure around SME involvement, business decision modeling methodologies can be applied to formalize the business problems to be solved and frame the role of machine learning in the solution.

Business Decision Modeling

Decision modeling creates a business blueprint of the decision-making process, allowing subject matter experts to directly structure and describe their needs. Decision models can be helpful because they put machine learning in context for subject matter experts. This allows the models to be integrated with the business rules, as well as helps the SMEs to fully understand decision contexts and the potential impact of model changes.

MLOps strategies that include a component of business decision modeling for subject matter experts can be an effective tool for ensuring that real-world machine learning model results are properly contextualized for those who don't have deep knowledge of how the underlying models themselves work.[1]

Subject matter experts have a role to play not only at the beginning of the ML model life cycle, but at the end (post-production) as well. Oftentimes, to understand if an ML model is performing well or as expected, data scientists need subject matter experts to close the feedback loop because traditional metrics (accuracy, precision, recall, etc.) are not enough.

For example, data scientists could build a simple churn prediction model that has very high accuracy in a production environment; however, marketing does not manage to prevent anyone from churning. From a business perspective, that means the model didn't work, and that's important information that needs to make its way back to those building the ML model so that they can find another possible solution, such as introducing uplift modeling that helps marketing better target potential churners who might be receptive to marketing messaging.

Given the role of SMEs in the ML model life cycle, it's critical when building MLOps processes to have an easy way for them to understand deployed model performance in business terms. That is, they need to understand not just model accuracy, precision, and recall, but the results or impact of the model on the business process identified up front. In addition, when there are unexpected shifts in performance, subject matter experts need a scalable way, through MLOps processes, to flag model results that don't align with business expectations.

On top of these explicit feedback mechanisms, more generally, MLOps should be built in a way that increases transparency for subject matter experts. That is, they should be able to use MLOps processes as a jumping-off point for exploring the data

---

1 Decision requirements models are based on Decision Model and Notation (*https://oreil.ly/6k5OT*), a framework for improving processes, effectively managing business rules projects, framing predictive analytics efforts, and ensuring decision support systems and dashboards are action-oriented.

pipelines behind the models, understanding what data is being used, how it's being transformed and enhanced, and what kind of machine learning techniques are being applied.

For subject matter experts who are also concerned with compliance of machine learning models with internal or external regulations, MLOps serves as an additional way to bring transparency and understanding to these processes. This includes being able to dig into individual decisions made by a model to understand why the model came to that decision. This should be complementary to statistical and aggregated feedback.

Ultimately, MLOps is most relevant for subject matter experts as a feedback mechanism and a platform for communication with data scientists about the models they are building. However, there are other MLOps needs as well—specifically around transparency, which ties into Responsible AI—that are relevant for subject matter experts and make them an important part of the MLOps picture.

Data Scientists

The needs of data scientists are the most critical ones to consider when building an MLOps strategy. To be sure, they have a lot to gain; data scientists at most organizations today often deal with siloed data, processes, and tools, making it difficult to effectively scale their efforts. MLOps is well positioned to change this.

Though most see data scientists' role in the ML model life cycle as strictly the model building portion, it is—or at least, it should be—much wider. From the very beginning, data scientists need to be involved with subject matter experts, understanding and helping to frame business problems in such a way that they can build a viable machine learning solution.

The reality is that this very first, critical step in the ML model life cycle is often the hardest. It's challenging particularly for data scientists because it's not where their training lies. Both formal and informal data science programs in universities and online heavily emphasize technical skills and not necessarily skills for communicating effectively with subject matter experts from the business side of the house, who usually are not intimately familiar with machine learning techniques. Once again, business decision modeling techniques can help here.

It's also a challenge because it can take time. For data scientists who want to dive in and get their hands dirty, spending weeks framing and outlining the problem before getting started on solving it can be torture. To top it off, data scientists are often siloed (physically, culturally, or both) from the core of the business and from subject matter experts, so they simply don't have access to an organizational infrastructure that facilitates easy collaboration between these profiles. Robust MLOps systems can help address some of these challenges.

After overcoming the first hurdle, depending on the organization, the project might get handed off to either data engineers or analysts to do some of the initial data gathering, preparation, and exploration. In some cases, data scientists themselves manage these parts of the ML model life cycle. But in any case, data scientists step back in when it comes time to build, test, robustify, and then deploy the model.

Following deployment, data scientists' roles include constantly assessing model quality to ensure the way it's working in production answers initial business questions or needs. The underlying question in many organizations is often whether data scientists monitor only the models they have had a hand in building or whether one person handles all monitoring. In the former scenario, what happens when there is staff turnover? In the latter scenario, building good MLOps practices is critical, as the person monitoring also needs to be able to quickly jump in and take action should the model drift and start negatively affecting the business. If they weren't the ones who built it, how can MLOps make this process seamless?

Operationalization and MLOps

Throughout 2018 and the beginning of 2019, operationalization was the key buzzword when it came to ML model life cycles and AI in the enterprise. Put simply, operationalization of data science is the process of pushing models to production and measuring their performance against business goals. So how does operationalization fit into the MLOps story? MLOps takes operationalization one step further, encompassing not just the push to production but the maintenance of those models—and the entire data pipeline—in production.

Though they are distinct, MLOps might be considered the new operationalization. That is, where many of the major hurdles for businesses to operationalize have disappeared, MLOps is the next frontier and presents the next big challenge for machine learning efforts in the enterprise.

All of the questions in the previous section lead directly here: data scientists' needs when it comes to MLOps. Starting from the end of the process and working backward, MLOps must provide data scientists with visibility into the performance of all deployed models as well as any models being A/B tested. But taking that one step further, it's not just about monitoring—it's also about action. Top-notch MLOps should allow data scientists the flexibility to select winning models from tests and easily deploy them.

Transparency is an overarching theme in MLOps, so it's no surprise that it's also a key need for data scientists. The ability to drill down into data pipelines and make quick assessments and adjustments (regardless of who originally built the model) is critical. Automated model packaging and delivery for quick and easy (yet safe) deployment to production is another important point for transparency, and it's a crucial component of MLOps, especially to bring data scientists together to a place of trust with software engineers and DevOps teams.

In addition to transparency, another theme for mastering MLOps—especially when it comes to meeting the needs of data scientists—is pure efficiency. In an enterprise setting, agility and speed matter. It's true for DevOps, and the story for MLOps is no different. Of course, data scientists can deploy, test, and monitor models in an ad hoc fashion. But they will spend enormous amounts of time reinventing the wheel with every single ML model, and that will never add up to scalable ML processes for the organization.

Data Engineers

Data pipelines are at the core of the ML model life cycle, and data engineers are, in turn, at the core of data pipelines. Because data pipelines can be abstract and complex, data engineers have a lot of efficiencies to gain from MLOps.

In large organizations, managing the flow of data, outside of the application of ML models, is a full-time job. Depending on the technical stack and organizational structure of the enterprise, data engineers might, therefore, be more focused on the databases themselves than on pipelines (especially if the company is leveraging data science and ML platforms that facilitate the visual building of pipelines by other data practitioners, like business analysts).

Ultimately, despite these slight variations in the role by an organization, the role of data engineers in the life cycle is to optimize the retrieval and use of data to eventually power ML models. Generally, this means working closely with business teams, particularly subject matter experts, to identify the right data for the project at hand and possibly also prepare it for use. On the other end, they work closely with data scientists to resolve any data plumbing issues that might cause a model to behave undesirably in production.

Given data engineers' central role in the ML model life cycle, underpinning both the building and monitoring portions, MLOps can bring significant efficiency gains. Data engineers require not only visibility into the performance of all models deployed in production, but the ability to take it one step further and directly drill down into individual data pipelines to address any underlying issues.

Ideally, for maximum efficiency for the data engineer profile (and for others as well, including data scientists), MLOps must not consist of simple monitoring, but be a bridge to underlying systems for investigating and tweaking ML models.

Software Engineers

It would be easy to exclude classical software engineers from MLOps consideration, but it is crucial from a wider organizational perspective to consider their needs to build a cohesive enterprise-wide strategy for machine learning.

Software engineers don't usually build ML models, but, on the other hand, most organizations are not *only* producing ML models, but classic software and applications as well. It's important that software engineers and data scientists work together to ensure the functioning of the larger system. After all, ML models aren't just stand-alone experiments; the machine learning code, training, testing, and deployment have to fit into the Continuous Integration/Continuous Delivery (CI/CD) pipelines that the rest of the software is using.

For example, consider a retail company that has built an ML-based recommendation engine for their website. The ML model was built by the data scientist, but to integrate it into the larger functioning of the site, software engineers will necessarily need to be involved. Similarly, software engineers are responsible for the maintenance of the website as a whole, and a large part of that includes the functioning of the ML models in production.

Given this interplay, software engineers need MLOps to provide them with model performance details as part of a larger picture of software application performance for the enterprise. MLOps is a way for data scientists and software engineers to speak the same language and have the same baseline understanding of how different models deployed across the silos of the enterprise are working together in production.

Other important features for software engineers include versioning, to be sure of what they are currently dealing with; automatic tests, to be as sure as possible that what they are currently dealing with is working; and the ability to work in parallel on the same application (thanks to a system that allows branches and merges like Git).

DevOps

MLOps was born out of DevOps principles, but that doesn't mean they can be run in parallel as completely separate and siloed systems.

DevOps teams have two primary roles in the ML model life cycle. First, they are the people conducting and building operational systems as well as tests to ensure security, performance, and availability of ML models. Second, they are responsible for CI/CD pipeline management. Both of these roles require tight collaboration with data scientists, data engineers, and data architects. Tight collaboration is, of course, easier said than done, but that is where MLOps can add value.

For DevOps teams, MLOps needs to be integrated into the larger DevOps strategy of the enterprise, bridging the gap between traditional CI/CD and modern ML. That means systems that are fundamentally complementary and that allow DevOps teams to automate tests for ML just as they can automate tests for traditional software.

Model Risk Manager/Auditor

In certain industries (particularly the financial services sector), the model risk management (MRM) function is crucial for regulatory compliance. But it's not only highly regulated industries that should be concerned or that should have a similar function; MRM can protect companies in any industry from catastrophic loss introduced by poorly performing ML models. What's more, audits play a role in many industries and can be labor intensive, which is where MLOps comes into the picture.

When it comes to the ML model life cycle, model risk managers play the critical role of analyzing not just model outcomes, but the initial goal and business questions ML models seek to resolve to minimize overall risk to the company. They should be involved along with subject matter experts at the very beginning of the life cycle to ensure that an automated, ML-based approach in and of itself doesn't present risk.

And, of course, they have a role to play in monitoring—their more traditional place in the model life cycle—to ensure that risks are kept at bay once models are in production. In between conception and monitoring, MRM also is a factor post-model development and preproduction, ensuring initial compliance with internal and external requirements.

MRM professionals and teams have a lot to gain from MLOps, because their work is often painstakingly manual. As MRM and the teams with which they work often use different tools, standardization can offer a huge leg up in the speed at which auditing and risk management can occur.

When it comes to specific MLOps needs, robust reporting tools on all models (whether they are currently in production or have been in production in the past) is the primary one. This reporting should include not just performance details, but the ability to see data lineage. Automated reporting adds an extra layer of efficiency for MRM and audit teams in MLOps systems and processes.

Machine Learning Architect

Traditional data architects are responsible for understanding the overall enterprise architecture and ensuring that it meets the requirements for data needs from across the business. They generally play a role in defining how data will be stored and consumed.

Today, demands on architects are much greater, and they often have to be knowledge-able not only on the ins and outs of data storage and consumption, but on how ML models work in tandem. This adds a lot of complexity to the role and increases their responsibility in the MLOps life cycle, and it's why in this section, we have called them machine learning architects instead of the more traditional "data architect" title.

Machine learning architects play a critical role in the ML model life cycle, ensuring a scalable and flexible environment for model pipelines. In addition, data teams need their expertise to introduce new technologies (when appropriate) that improve ML model performance in production. It is for this reason that the data architect title isn't enough; they need to have an intimate understanding of machine learning, not just enterprise architecture, to play this key role in the ML model life cycle.

This role requires collaboration across the enterprise, from data scientists and engi-neers to DevOps and software engineers. Without a complete understanding of the needs of each of these people and teams, machine learning architects cannot properly allocate resources to ensure optimal performance of ML models in production.

When it comes to MLOps, the machine learning architects' role is about having a centralized view of resource allocation. As they have a strategic, tactical role, they need an overview of the situation to identify bottlenecks and use that information to find long-term improvements. Their role is one of pinpointing possible new technol-ogy or infrastructure for investment, not necessarily operational quick fixes that don't address the heart of the scalability of the system.

Closing Thoughts

MLOps isn't just for data scientists; a diverse group of experts across the organization has a role to play not only in the ML model life cycle, but the MLOps strategy as well. In fact, each person—from the subject matter expert on the business side to the most technical machine learning architect—plays a critical part in the maintenance of ML models in production. This is ultimately important not only to ensure the best possi-ble results from ML models (good results generally lead to more trust in ML-based systems as well as increased budget to build more), but, perhaps more pointedly, to protect the business from the risks outlined in Chapter 1.

CHAPTER 3

Key MLOps Features

Mark Treveil

MLOps affects many different roles across the organization and, in turn, many parts of the machine learning life cycle. This chapter introduces the five key components of MLOps (development, deployment, monitoring, iteration, and governance) at a high level as a foundation for Chapters 4 through 8, which delve into the more technical details and requirements of these components.

A Primer on Machine Learning

To understand the key features of MLOps, it's essential first to understand how machine learning works and be intimately familiar with its specificities. Though often overlooked in its role as a part of MLOps, ultimately algorithm selection (or how machine learning models are built) can have a direct impact on MLOps processes.

At its core, machine learning is the science of computer algorithms that automatically learn and improve from experience rather than being explicitly programmed. The algorithms analyze sample data, known as training data, to build a software model that can make predictions.

For example, an image recognition model might be able to identify the type of electricity meter from a photograph by searching for key patterns in the image that distinguish each type of meter. Another example is an insurance recommender model, which might suggest additional insurance products that a specific existing customer is most likely to buy based on the previous behavior of similar customers.

When faced with unseen data, be it a photo or a customer, the ML model uses what it has learned from previous data to make the best prediction it can based on the assumption that the unseen data is somehow related to the previous data.

ML algorithms use a wide range of mathematical techniques, and the models can take many different forms, from simple decision trees to logistic regression algorithms to much more complex deep learning models (see "What Is a Machine Learning Model?" on page 42 for details).

Model Development

Let's take a deeper look into ML model development as a whole for an even more complete understanding of its components, all of which can have an impact on MLOps after deployment.

Establishing Business Objectives

The process of developing a machine learning model typically starts with a business objective, which can be as simple as reducing fraudulent transactions to < 0.1% or having the ability to identify people's faces on their social media photos. Business objectives naturally come with performance targets, technical infrastructure requirements, and cost constraints; all of these factors can be captured as key performance indicators, or KPIs, which will ultimately enable the business performance of models in production to be monitored.

It's important to recognize that ML projects don't happen in a vacuum. They are generally part of a larger project that in turn impacts technologies, processes, and people. That means part of establishing objectives also includes change management, which may even provide some guidance for how the ML model should be built. For example, the required degree of transparency will strongly influence the choice of algorithms and may drive the need to provide explanations together with predictions so that predictions are turned into valuable decisions at the business level.

Data Sources and Exploratory Data Analysis

With clear business objectives defined, it is time to bring together subject matter experts and data scientists to begin the journey of developing the ML model. This starts with the search for suitable input data. Finding data sounds simple, but in practice, it can be the most arduous part of the journey.

Key questions for finding data to build ML models include:

- What relevant datasets are available?
- Is this data sufficiently accurate and reliable?
- How can stakeholders get access to this data?
- What data properties (known as *features*) can be made available by combining multiple sources of data?

- Will this data be available in real time?
- Is there a need to label some of the data with the "ground truth" that is to be predicted, or does unsupervised learning make sense? If so, how much will this cost in terms of time and resources?
- What platform should be used?
- How will data be updated once the model is deployed?
- Will the use of the model itself reduce the representativeness of the data?
- How will the KPIs, which were established along with the business objectives, be measured?

The constraints of data governance bring even more questions, including:

- Can the selected datasets be used for this purpose?
- What are the terms of use?
- Is there personally identifiable information (PII) that must be redacted or anonymized?
- Are there features, such as gender, that legally cannot be used in this business context?
- Are minority populations sufficiently well represented that the model has equivalent performances on each group?

Since data is the essential ingredient to power ML algorithms, it always helps to build an understanding of the patterns in data before attempting to train models. Exploratory data analysis (EDA) techniques can help build hypotheses about the data, identify data cleaning requirements, and inform the process of selecting potentially significant features. EDA can be carried out visually for intuitive insight and statistically if more rigor is required.

Feature Engineering and Selection

EDA leads naturally into feature engineering and feature selection. Feature engineering is the process of taking raw data from the selected datasets and transforming it into "features" that better represent the underlying problem to be solved. "Features" are arrays of numbers of fixed size, as it is the only object that ML algorithms understand. Feature engineering includes data cleansing, which can represent the largest part of an ML project in terms of time spent. For details, see "Feature Engineering and Selection" on page 47.

Training and Evaluation

After data preparation by way of feature engineering and selection, the next step is training. The process of training and optimizing a new ML model is iterative; several algorithms may be tested, features can be automatically generated, feature selections may be adapted, and algorithm hyperparameters tuned. In addition to—or in many cases because of—its iterative nature, training is also the most intensive step of the ML model life cycle when it comes to computing power.

Keeping track of the results of each experiment when iterating becomes complex quickly. Nothing is more frustrating to data scientists than not being able to re-create the best results because they cannot remember the precise configuration. An experiment tracking tool can greatly simplify the process of remembering the data, the features selection, and model parameters alongside the performance metrics. These enable experiments to be compared side-by-side, highlighting the differences in performance.

Deciding what is the best solution requires both quantitative criteria, such as accuracy or average error, and qualitative criteria regarding the explainability of the algorithm or its ease of deployment.

Reproducibility

While many experiments may be short-lived, significant versions of a model need to be saved for possible later use. The challenge here is reproducibility, which is an important concept in experimental science in general. The aim in ML is to save enough information about the environment the model was developed in so that the model can be reproduced with the same results from scratch.

Without reproducibility, data scientists have little chance of being able to confidently iterate on models, and worse, they are unlikely to be able to hand over the model to DevOps to see if what was created in the lab can be faithfully reproduced in production. True reproducibility requires version control of all the assets and parameters involved, including the data used to train and evaluate the model, as well as a record of the software environment (see "Version Management and Reproducibility" on page 56 for details).

Responsible AI

Being able to reproduce the model is only part of the operationalization challenge; the DevOps team also needs to understand how to verify the model (i.e., what does the model do, how should it be tested, and what are the expected results?). Those in highly regulated industries are likely required to document even more detail, including how the model was built and how it was tuned. In critical cases, the model may be independently recoded and rebuilt.

Documentation is still the standard solution to this communication challenge. Automated model document generation, whereby a tool automatically creates documentation associated with any trained model, can make the task less onerous. But in almost all cases, some documentation will need to be written by hand to explain the choices made.

It is a fundamental consequence of their statistical nature that ML models are challenging to understand. While model algorithms come with standard performance measures to assess their efficacy, these don't explain how the predictions are made. The "how" is important as a way to sanity-check the model or help better engineer features, and it may be necessary to ensure that fairness requirements (e.g., around features like sex, age, or race) have been met. This is the field of explainability, which is connected to Responsible AI as discussed in Chapter 1 and which will be discussed in further detail in Chapter 4.

Explainability techniques are becoming increasingly important as global concerns grow about the impact of unbridled AI. They offer a way to mitigate uncertainty and help prevent unintended consequences. The techniques most commonly used today include:

- Partial dependence plots, which look at the marginal impact of features on the predicted outcome
- Subpopulation analyses, which look at how the model treats specific subpopulations and that are the basis of many fairness analyses
- Individual model predictions, such as Shapley values (*https://oreil.ly/OC8OK*), which explain how the value of each feature contributes to a specific prediction
- What-if analysis, which helps the ML model user to understand the sensitivity of the prediction to its inputs

As we've seen in this section, even though model development happens very early on, it's still an important place to incorporate MLOps practices. Any MLOps work done up front during the model development stage will make the models easier to manage down the line (especially when pushing to production).

Productionalization and Deployment

Productionalizing and deploying models is a key component of MLOps that presents an entirely different set of technical challenges than developing the model. It is the domain of the software engineer and the DevOps team, and the organizational challenges in managing the information exchange between the data scientists and these teams must not be underestimated. As touched on in Chapter 1, without effective collaboration between the teams, delays or failures to deploy are inevitable.

Model Deployment Types and Contents

To understand what happens in these phases, it's helpful to take a step back and ask: what exactly is going into production, and what does a model consist of? There are commonly two types of model deployment:

Model-as-a-service, or live-scoring model
> Typically the model is deployed into a simple framework to provide a REST API endpoint (the means from which the API can access the resources it needs to perform the task) that responds to requests in real time.

Embedded model
> Here the model is packaged into an application, which is then published. A common example is an application that provides batch-scoring of requests.

What to-be-deployed models consist of depends, of course, on the technology chosen, but typically they comprise a set of code (commonly Python, R, or Java) and data artifacts. Any of these can have version dependencies on runtimes and packages that need to match in the production environment because the use of different versions may cause model predictions to differ.

One approach to reducing dependencies on the production environment is to export the model to a portable format such as PMML, PFA, ONNX, or POJO. These aim to improve model portability between systems and simplify deployment. However, they come at a cost: each format supports a limited range of algorithms, and sometimes the portable models behave in subtly different ways than the original. Whether or not to use a portable format is a choice to be made based on a thorough understanding of the technological and business context.

Containerization

Containerization is an increasingly popular solution to the headaches of dependencies when deploying ML models. Container technologies such as Docker are lightweight alternatives to virtual machines, allowing applications to be deployed in independent, self-contained environments, matching the exact requirements of each model.

They also enable new models to be seamlessly deployed using the blue-green deployment technique.[1] Compute resources for models can be scaled elastically using multiple containers, too. Orchestrating many containers is the role of technologies such as Kubernetes and can be used both in the cloud and on-premise.

---

[1] Describing the blue-green deployment technique will require more space than we have here. For more information, see Martin Fowler's blog (*https://oreil.ly/Uuobx*).

Model Deployment Requirements

So what about the productionalization process between completing model development and physically deploying into production—what needs to be addressed? One
thing is for sure: rapid, automated deployment is always preferred to labor-intensive
processes.

For short-lifetime, self-service applications, there often isn't much need to worry
about testing and validation. If the maximum resource demands of the model can be
securely capped by technologies such as Linux cgroups, then a fully automated single-
step push-to-production may be entirely adequate. It is even possible to handle simple user interfaces with frameworks like Flask when using this lightweight
deployment mode. Along with integrated data science and machine learning platforms, some business rule management systems may also allow some sort of autonomous deployment of basic ML models.

In customer-facing, mission-critical use cases, a more robust CI/CD pipeline is
required. This typically involves:

1. Ensuring all coding, documentation and sign-off standards have been met
2. Re-creating the model in something approaching the production environment
3. Revalidating the model accuracy
4. Performing explainability checks
5. Ensuring all governance requirements have been met
6. Checking the quality of any data artifacts
7. Testing resource usage under load
8. Embedding into a more complex application, including integration tests

In heavily regulated industries (e.g., finance and pharmaceuticals), governance and
regulatory checks will be extensive and are likely to involve manual intervention. The
desire in MLOps, just as in DevOps, is to automate the CI/CD pipeline as far as possible. This not only speeds up the deployment process, but it enables more extensive
regression testing and reduces the likelihood of errors in the deployment.

Monitoring

Once a model is deployed to production, it is crucial that it continue to perform well
over time. But good performance means different things to different people, in particular to the DevOps team, to data scientists, and to the business.

DevOps Concerns

The concerns of the DevOps team are very familiar and include questions like:

- Is the model getting the job done quickly enough?
- Is it using a sensible amount of memory and processing time?

This is traditional IT performance monitoring, and DevOps teams know how to do this well already. The resource demands of ML models are not so different from traditional software in this respect.

Scalability of compute resources can be an important consideration, for example, if you are retraining models in production. Deep learning models have greater resource demands than much simpler decision trees. But overall, the existing expertise in DevOps teams for monitoring and managing resources can be readily applied to ML models.

Data Scientist Concerns

The data scientist is interested in monitoring ML models for a new, more challenging reason: they can degrade over time, since ML models are effectively models of the data they were trained on. This is not a problem faced by traditional software, but it is inherent to machine learning. ML mathematics builds a concise representation of the important patterns in the training data with the hope that this is a good reflection of the real world. If the training data reflects the real world well, then the model should be accurate and, thus, useful.

But the real world doesn't stand still. The training data used to build a fraud detection model six months ago won't reflect a new type of fraud that has started to occur in the last three months. If a given website starts to attract an increasingly younger user base, then a model that generates advertisements is likely to produce less and less relevant adverts. At some point, the performance will become unacceptable, and model retraining becomes necessary. How soon models need to be retrained depends on how fast the real world is changing and how accurate the model needs to be, but also, importantly, on how easy it is to build and deploy a better model.

But first, how can data scientists tell a model's performance is degrading? It's not always easy. There are two common approaches, one based on ground truth and the other on input drift.

Ground truth

The ground truth, put simply, is the correct answer to the question that the model was asked to solve—for example, "Is this credit card transaction actually fraudulent?"

In knowing the ground truth for all the predictions a model has made, one can judge how well that model is performing.

Sometimes ground truth is obtained rapidly after a prediction—for example, in models that decide which advertisements to display to a user on a web page. The user is likely to click on the advertisements within seconds, or not at all. However, in many use cases, obtaining the ground truth is much slower. If a model predicts that a transaction is fraudulent, how can this be confirmed? In some cases, verification may only take a few minutes, such as a phone call placed to the cardholder. But what about the transactions the model thought were OK but actually weren't? The best hope is that they will be reported by the cardholder when they review their monthly transactions, but this could happen up to a month after the event (or not at all).

In the fraud example, ground truth isn't going to enable data science teams to monitor performance accurately on a daily basis. If the situation requires rapid feedback, then input drift may be a better approach.

Input drift

Input drift is based on the principle that a model is only going to predict accurately if the data it was trained on is an accurate reflection of the real world. So if a comparison of recent requests to a deployed model against the training data shows distinct differences, then there is a strong likelihood that the model performance is compromised. This is the basis of input drift monitoring. The beauty of this approach is that all the data required for this test already exists, so there is no need to wait for ground truth or any other information.

Identifying drift is one of the most important components of an adaptable MLOps strategy, and one that can bring agility to the organization's enterprise AI efforts overall. Chapter 7 will go into more technical depth about data scientists' concerns when it comes to model monitoring.

Business Concerns

The business has a holistic outlook on monitoring, and some of its concerns might include questions like:

- Is the model delivering value to the enterprise?
- Do the benefits of the model outweigh the cost of developing and deploying it? (And how can we measure this?)

The KPIs identified for the original business objective are one part of this process. Where possible, these should be monitored automatically, but this is rarely trivial. The objective of reducing fraud to less than 0.1% of transactions in our previous example is reliant on establishing the ground truth. But even monitoring this doesn't answer the question: what is the net gain to the business in dollars?

This is an age-old challenge for software, and with ever-increasing expenditure on ML, the pressure for data scientists to demonstrate value is only going to grow. In the absence of a "dollar-o-meter," effectively monitoring the business KPIs is the best option available (see "Design and Manage Experiments" on page 138). The choice of the baseline is important here and should ideally allow for differentiation of the value of the ML subproject specifically, rather than that of the global project. For example, the ML performance can be assessed with respect to a rule-based decision model based on subject matter expertise to set apart the contribution of decision automation and of ML per se.

Iteration and Life Cycle

Developing and deploying improved versions of a model is an essential part of the MLOps life cycle, and one of the more challenging. There are various reasons to develop a new model version, one of which is model performance degradation due to model drift, as discussed in the prior section. Sometimes there is a need to reflect refined business objectives and KPIs, and other times, it's just that the data scientists have come up with a better way to design the model.

Iteration

In some fast-moving business environments, new training data becomes available every day. Daily retraining and redeployment of the model are often automated to ensure that the model reflects recent experience as closely as possible.

Retraining an existing model with the latest training data is the simplest scenario for iterating a new model version. But while there are no changes to feature selection or algorithm, there are still plenty of pitfalls. In particular:

- Does the new training data look as expected? Automated validation of the new data through predefined metrics and checks is essential.
- Is the data complete and consistent?
- Are the distributions of features broadly similar to those in the previous training set? Remember that the goal is to refine the model, not radically change it.

With a new model version built, the next step is to compare the metrics with the current live model version. Doing so requires evaluating both models on the same development dataset, whether it be the previous or latest version. If metrics and checks suggest a wide variation between the models, automated scripts should not be redeployed, and manual intervention should be sought.

Even in the "simple" automated retraining scenario with new training data, there is a need for multiple development datasets based on scoring data reconciliation (with ground truth when it becomes available), data cleaning and validation, the previous model version, and a set of carefully considered checks. Retraining in other scenarios is likely to be even more complicated, rendering automated redeployment unlikely.

As an example, consider retraining motivated by the detection of significant input drift. How can the model be improved? If new training data is available, then retraining with this data is the action with the highest cost-benefit ratio, and it may suffice. However, in environments where it's slow to obtain the ground truth, there may be little new labeled data.

This case requires direct invention from data scientists who need to understand the cause of the drift and work out how the existing training data could be adjusted to more accurately reflect the latest input data. Evaluating a model generated by such changes is difficult. The data scientist has to spend time assessing the situation—time that increases with the amount of modeling debt—as well as estimate the potential impact on performance and design custom mitigation measures. For example, removing a specific feature or sampling the existing rows of training data may lead to a better-tuned model.

The Feedback Loop

In large enterprises, DevOps best practices typically dictate that the live model scoring environment and the model retraining environment are distinct. As a result, the evaluation of a new model version on the retraining environment is likely to be compromised.

One approach to mitigating this uncertainty is shadow testing, where the new model version is deployed into the live environment alongside the existing model. All live scoring is handled by the incumbent model version, but each new request is then scored again by the new model version and the results logged, but not returned to the requestor. Once sufficient requests have been scored by both versions, the results can be compared statistically. Shadow scoring also gives more visibility to the SMEs on the future versions of the model and may thus allow for a smoother transition.

In the advertisement generation model previously discussed, it is impossible to tell if the ads selected by the model are good or bad without allowing the end user the chance to click on them. In this use case, shadow testing has limited benefits, and A/B testing is more common.

In A/B testing, both models are deployed into the live environment, but input requests are split between the two models. Each request is processed by one or the other model, not both. Results from the two models are logged for analysis (but never for the same request). Drawing statistically meaningful conclusions from an A/B test requires careful planning of the test.

Chapter 7 will cover the how-to of A/B testing in more detail, but as a preview, the simplest form of A/B testing is often referred to as a fixed-horizon test. That's because in the search for a statistically meaningful conclusion, one has to wait until the carefully predetermined number of samples have been tested. "Peeking" at the result before the test is finished is unreliable. However, if the test is running live in a commercial environment, every bad prediction is likely to cost money, so not being able to stop a test early could be expensive.

Bayesian, and in particular multi-armed bandit, tests are an increasingly popular alternative to the "frequentist" fixed-horizon test, with the aim of drawing conclusions more quickly. Multi-armed bandit testing is adaptive: the algorithm that decides the split between models adapts according to live results and reduces the workload of underperforming models. While multi-armed bandit testing is more complex, it can reduce the business cost of sending traffic to a poorly performing model.

Iterating on the Edge

Iterating on an ML model deployed to millions of devices, such as smartphones, sensors, or cars, presents different challenges to iteration in a corporate IT environment. One approach is to relay all the feedback from the millions of model instances to a central point and perform training centrally. Tesla's autopilot system (*https://oreil.ly/7jWqk*), running in more than 500,000 cars, does exactly this. Full retraining of their 50 or so neural networks takes 70,000 GPU hours.

Google has taken a different approach with its smartphone keyboard software, GBoard (*https://oreil.ly/79xaw*). Instead of centralized retraining, every smartphone retrains the model locally and sends a summary of the improvements it has found to Google centrally. These improvements from every device are averaged and the shared model updated. This federated learning approach means that an individual user's personal data doesn't need to be collected centrally, the improved model on each phone can be used immediately, and the overall power consumption goes down.

Governance

Governance is the set of controls placed on a business to ensure that it delivers on its responsibilities to all stakeholders, from shareholders and employees to the public and national governments. These responsibilities include financial, legal, and ethical obligations. Underpinning all three of these is the fundamental principle of fairness.

Legal obligations are the easiest to understand. Businesses were constrained by regulations long before the advent of machine learning. Many regulations target specific industries; for example, financial regulations aim to protect the public and wider economy from finance mismanagement and fraud, while pharmaceutical industries must comply with rules to safeguard the health of the public. Business practice is impacted by broader legislation to protect vulnerable sectors of society and to ensure a level playing field on criteria such as sex, race, age, or religion.

Recently, governments across the world have imposed regulations to protect the public from the impact of the use of personal data by businesses. The 2016 EU General Data Protection Regulation (GDPR) and the 2018 California Consumer Privacy Act (CCPA) typify this trend, and their impact on ML—with its total dependency on data —has been immense. For example, GDPR attempts to protect personal data from industrial misuse with a goal of limiting the potential discrimination against individuals.

GDPR Principles

The GDPR sets out principles for the processing of personal data, and it's worth noting that the CCPA was built to closely mirror its principles, though it does have some significant differences.[2] Processing includes the collection, storage, alteration, and use of personal data. These principles are:

- Lawfulness, fairness, and transparency
- Purpose limitation
- Data minimization
- Accuracy
- Storage limitation
- Integrity and confidentiality (security)
- Accountability

Governments are now starting to turn their regulatory eye to ML specifically, hoping to mitigate the negative impact of its use. The European Union is leading the way with planned legislation to define the acceptable uses of various forms of AI. This is not necessarily about reducing use; for example, it may enable beneficial applications of facial recognition technology that are currently restricted by data privacy regulations. But what is clear is that businesses will have to take heed of yet more regulation when applying ML.

---

2 Delve into the differences between GDPR and CCPA (*https://oreil.ly/zS7o6*).

Do businesses care about moral responsibilities to society, beyond formal legislation? Increasingly, the answer is yes, as seen in the current development of environmental, social, and governance (ESG) performance indicators. Trust matters to consumers, and a lack of trust is bad for business. With increasing public activism on the subject, businesses are engaging with ideas of Responsible AI, the ethical, transparent, and accountable application of AI technology. Trust matters to shareholders, too, and full disclosure of ML risks is on its way.

Applying good governance to MLOPs is challenging. The processes are complex, the technology is opaque, and the dependence on data is fundamental. Governance initiatives in MLOps broadly fall into one of two categories:

Data governance
    A framework for ensuring appropriate use and management of data

Process governance
    The use of well-defined processes to ensure all governance considerations have been addressed at the correct point in the life cycle of the model and that a full and accurate record has been kept

Data Governance

Data governance concerns itself with the data being used, especially that for model training, and it can address questions like:

- What is the data's provenance?
- How was the original data collected and under what terms of use?
- Is the data accurate and up to date?
- Is there PII or other forms of sensitive data that should not be used?

ML projects usually involve significant pipelines, consisting of data cleaning, combination, and transformation steps. Understanding the data lineage is complex, especially at the feature level, but it is essential for compliance with GDPR-style regulations. How can teams—and more broadly organizations, as it matters at the top as well—be sure that no PII is used to train a given model? Anonymizing or pseudo-anonymizing data is not always a sufficient solution to managing personal information. If these processes are not performed correctly, it can still be possible to single out an individual and their data, contrary to the requirements of GDPR.[3]

---

3 For more on anonymization, pseudo-anonymization, and why they don't solve all data privacy woes, we recommend *Executing Data Privacy-Compliant Data Projects* by Dataiku (*https://oreil.ly/bK1Yu*).

Inappropriate biases in models can arise quite accidentally despite the best intentions of data scientists. An ML recruitment model famously discriminated against women by identifying that certain schools—all-female schools—were less well represented in the company's upper management, which reflected the historical dominance of men in the organization.[4] The point is that making predictions based on experience is a powerful technique, but sometimes the consequences are not only counter-productive, but illegal.

Data governance tools that can address these problems are in their infancy. Most focus on answering these two questions about data lineage:

- Where did the information in this dataset come from, and what does this tell me about how I can use it?
- How is this dataset used, and if I change it in some way, what are the implications downstream?

Neither question is easy to answer fully and accurately in real-world data preparation pipelines. For example, if a data scientist writes a Python function to in-memory process several input datasets and output a single dataset, how can one be sure from what information each cell of the new dataset was derived?

Process Governance

Process governance focuses on formalizing the steps in the MLOps process and associating actions with them. Typically these actions are reviews, sign-offs, and the capture of supporting materials, such as documentation. The aim is twofold:

- To ensure every governance-related consideration is made at the correct time and correctly acted upon. For example, models should not be deployed to production until all validation checks have been passed.
- To enable oversight from outside of the strict MLOps process. Auditors, risk managers, compliance officers, and the business as a whole all have an interest in being able to track progress and review decisions at a later stage.

Effective implementation of process governance is hard:

- Formal processes for the ML life cycle are rarely easy to define accurately. The understanding of the complete process is usually spread across the many teams involved, often with no one person having a detailed understanding of it as a whole.

---

4 In 2018, Amazon famously scrapped an AI recruiting tool because of its bias against women (*https://oreil.ly/tI5Sy*).

- For the process to be applied successfully, every team must be willing to adopt it wholeheartedly.

- If the process is just too heavy-weight for some use-cases, teams will certainly subvert it, and much of the benefit will be lost.

Today, process governance is most commonly found in organizations with a traditionally heavy burden of regulation and compliance, such as finance. Outside of these, it is rare. With ML creeping into all spheres of commercial activity and with rising concern about Responsible AI, we will need new and innovative solutions to this problem that can work for all businesses.

Closing Thoughts

Given this overview of features required for and processes affected by MLOps, it's clearly not something data teams—or even the data-driven organization at large—can ignore. Nor is it an item to check off of a list ("yes, we do MLOps!"), but rather a complex interplay between technologies, processes, and people that requires discipline and time to do correctly.

The following chapters go deeper into each of the ML model life cycle components at play in MLOps, providing a look at how each should be done to get closer to the ideal MLOps implementation.

MLOps: How

PART II
MLOps: How

CHAPTER 4

Developing Models

Adrien Lavoillotte

Anyone who wants to be serious about MLOps needs to have at least a cursory understanding of the model development process, which is presented in Figure 4-1 as an element of the larger ML project life cycle. Depending on the situation, the model development process can range from quite simple to extremely complex, and it dictates the constraints of subsequent usage, monitoring, and maintenance of models.

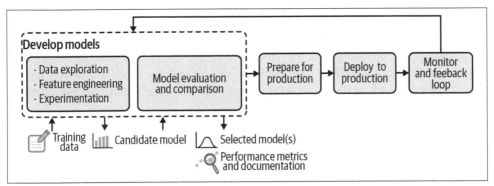

Figure 4-1. Model development highlighted in the larger context of the ML project life cycle

The implications of the data collection process on the rest of the model's life is quite straightforward, and one easily sees how a model can become stale. For other parts of the model, the effects may be less obvious.

For example, take feature creation, where feeding a date to the model versus a flag indicating whether the day is a public holiday may make a big difference in performance, but also comes with significantly different constraints on updating the model. Or consider how the metrics used for evaluating and comparing models may enable automatic switching to the best possible version down the line, should the situation require it.

This chapter therefore covers the basics of model development, specifically in the context of MLOps, that is, how models might be built and developed in ways that make MLOps considerations easier to implement down the line.

What Is a Machine Learning Model?

Machine learning models are leveraged both in academia and in the real world (i.e., business contexts), so it's important to distinguish what they represent in theory versus how they are implemented in practice. Let's dive into both, building on what we've already seen in Chapter 3.

In Theory

A machine learning model is a projection of reality; that is, it's a partial and approximate representation of some aspect (or aspects) of a real thing or process. Which aspects are represented often depends on what is available and useful. A machine learning model, once trained, boils down a mathematical formula that yields a result when fed some inputs—say, a probability estimation of some event happening or the estimated value of a raw number.

Machine learning models are based on statistical theory, and machine learning algorithms are the tools that build models from training data. Their goal is to find a synthetic representation of the data they are fed, and this data represents the world as it was at the time of collection. Therefore, machine learning models can be used to make predictions when the future looks like the past, because their synthetic representation is still valid.

Generalization Capacity

Machine learning models' ability to accurately predict for cases that are not exactly like the input data is called their *generalization capacity*. Even when they yield outputs like horses with zebra stripes[1] that do not exist in training datasets, they do it by modeling a probability distribution that allows them to have this kind of surprising generalization capacity.

---

1 CycleGAN is the implementation of recent research by Jun-Yan Zhu, Taesung Park, Phillip Isola, and Alexei A. Efros (*https://oreil.ly/7A_qd*).

An often-used example for how machine learning models can predict and generalize is the price of a house. Of course, the selling price of a house will depend on too many factors too complex to model precisely, but getting close enough to be useful is not so difficult. The input data for that model may be things inherent to the house like surface area, number of bedrooms and bathrooms, year of construction, location, etc., but also other more contextual information like the state of the housing market at the time of sale, whether the seller is in a hurry, and so on. With complete enough historical data, and provided the market conditions do not change too much, an algorithm can compute a formula that provides a reasonable estimate.

Another frequent example is a health diagnosis or prediction that someone will develop a certain disease within a given timeframe. This kind of classification model often outputs the probability of some event, sometimes also with a confidence interval.

In Practice

A model is the set of parameters necessary to rebuild and apply the formula. It is usually stateless and deterministic (i.e., the same inputs always give the same outputs, with some exceptions; see "Online Learning" on page 88).

This includes the parameters of the end formula itself, but it also includes all the transformations to go from the input data that will be fed to the model to the end formula that will yield a value plus the possible derived data (like a classification or a decision). Given this description in practice, it usually does not make a difference whether the model is ML-based or not: it is just a computable mathematical function applied to the input data, one row at a time.

In the house price case, for instance, it may not be practical to gather enough pricing data for every zip code to get a model that's accurate enough in all target locations. Instead, maybe the zip codes will be replaced with some derived inputs that are deemed to have the most influence on price—say, average income, population density, or proximity to some amenities. But since end users will continue to input the zip code and not these derived inputs, for all intents and purposes, all of this transformation is also part of the pricing model.

Outputs can also be richer than a single number. A system that detects fraud, for example, will often provide some kind of probability (and in some cases maybe also a confidence interval) rather than a binary answer. Depending on the acceptability of fraud and the cost of subsequent verification or denial of the transaction, it may be set up to only classify fraudulent instances where the probability reaches some fine-tuned threshold. Some models even include recommendations or decisions, such as which product to show a visitor to maximize spending or which treatment provides the most probable recovery.

All of these transformations and associated data are part of the model to some degree; however, this does not mean they are always bundled in a monolithic package, as one single artifact compiled together. This could quickly get unwieldy, and, in addition, some parts of this information come with varying constraints (different refresh rates, external sources, etc.).

Required Components

Building a machine learning model requires many components as outlined in Table 4-1.

Table 4-1. Required components of a machine learning model

ML component	Description
Training data	Training data is usually labeled for the prediction case with examples of what is being modeled (supervised learning). It might sound obvious, but it's important to have *good* training data. An illustrative example of when this was not the case was data from damaged planes during World War II (*https://oreil.ly/sssfA*), which suffered from survivor bias and therefore was not good training data.
A performance metric	A performance metric is what the model being developed seeks to optimize. It should be chosen carefully to avoid unintended consequences, like the cobra effect (*https://oreil.ly/DYOss*) (named for a famous anecdote, where a reward for dead cobras led some to breed them). For example, if 95% of the data has class A, optimizing for raw accuracy may produce a model that always predicts A and is 95% accurate.
ML algorithm	There are a variety of models that work in various ways and have different pros and cons. It is important to note that some algorithms are more suited to certain tasks than others, but their selection also depends on what needs to be prioritized: performance, stability, interpretability, computation cost, etc.
Hyperparameters	Hyperparameters are configurations for ML algorithms. The algorithm contains the basic formula, the *parameters* it learns are the operations and operands that make up this formula for that particular prediction task, and the *hyperparameters* are the ways that the algorithm may go to find these parameters. For example, in a decision tree (where data continues to be split in two according to what looks to be the best predictor in the subset that reached this path), one hyperparameter is the depth of the tree (i.e., the number of splits).
Evaluation dataset	When using labeled data, an evaluation dataset that is different from the training set will be required to evaluate how the model performs on unseen data (i.e., how well it can generalize).

The sheer number and complexity of each individual component is part of what can make good MLOps a challenging undertaking. But the complexity doesn't stop here, as algorithm choice is yet another piece of the puzzle.

Different ML Algorithms, Different MLOps Challenges

What ML algorithms all have in common is that they model patterns in past data to make inferences, and the quality and relevance of this experience are the key factors in their effectiveness. Where they differ is that each style of algorithm has specific characteristics and presents different challenges in MLOps (outlined in Table 4-2).

Table 4-2. MLOps considerations by algorithm type

Algorithm type	Name	MLOps considerations
Linear	Linear regression	There is a tendency for overfitting.
	Logistic regression	There is a tendency for overfitting.
Tree-based	Decision tree	Can be unstable—small changes in data can lead to a large change in the structure of the optimal decision tree.
	Random forest	Predictions can be difficult to understand, which is challenging from a Responsible AI perspective. Random forest models can also be relatively slow to output predictions, which can present challenges for applications.
	Gradient boosting	Like random forest, predictions can be difficult to understand. Also, a small change in the feature or training set can create radical changes in the model.
Deep learning	Neural networks	In terms of interpretability, deep learning models are almost impossible to understand. Deep learning algorithms, including neural networks, are also extremely slow to train and require a lot of power (and data). Is it worth the resources, or would a simpler model work just as well?

Some ML algorithms can best support specific use cases, but governance considerations may also play a part in the choice of algorithm. In particular, highly regulated environments where decisions must be explained (e.g., financial services) cannot use opaque algorithms such as neural networks; rather, they have to favor simpler techniques, such as decision trees. In many use cases, it's not so much a trade-off on performance but rather a trade-off on cost. That is, simpler techniques usually require more costly manual feature engineering to reach the same level of performance as more complex techniques.

Computing Power

When talking about components of machine learning model development, it's impossible to ignore computing power. Some say planes fly thanks to human ingenuity, but it's also thanks to a lot of fuel. This holds true with machine learning as well: its development is inversely proportional to the cost of computing power.

From hand-computed linear regression of the early twentieth century to today's largest deep learning models, new algorithms arose when the required computing power became available. For example, mainstream algorithms like random forest and gradient boosting both require a computing power that was expensive 20 years ago.

In exchange, they brought an ease of use that considerably lowered the cost of developing ML models, thus putting new use cases within the reach of the average organization. The decrease in the cost of data also helped, but it was not the first driver: very few algorithms leverage big data technology in which both data and computation are distributed over a large number of computers; rather, most of them still operate with all the training data in memory.

Data Exploration

When data scientists or analysts consider data sources to train a model, they need to first get a grasp of what that data looks like. Even a model trained using the most effective algorithm is only as good as its training data. At this stage, a number of issues can prevent all or part of the data from being useful, including incompleteness, inaccuracy, inconsistency, etc.

Examples of such processes can include:

- Documenting how the data was collected and what assumptions were already made
- Looking at summarizing statistics of the data: What is the domain of each column? Are there some rows with missing values? Obvious mistakes? Strange outliers? No outliers at all?
- Taking a closer look at the distribution of the data
- Cleaning, filling, reshaping, filtering, clipping, sampling, etc.
- Checking correlations between the different columns, running statistical tests on some subpopulations, fitting distribution curves
- Comparing that data to other data or models in the literature: Is there some usual information that seems to be missing? Is this data comparably distributed?

Of course, domain knowledge is required to make informed decisions during this exploration. Some oddities may be hard to spot without specific insight, and assumptions made can have consequences that are not obvious to the untrained eye. Industrial sensor data is a good example: unless the data scientist is also a mechanical engineer or expert in the equipment, they might not know what constitutes normal versus strange outliers for a particular machine.

Feature Engineering and Selection

Features are how data is presented to a model, serving to inform that model on things it may not infer by itself. This table provides examples of how features may be engineered:

Feature engineering category	Description
Derivatives	Infer new information from existing information—e.g., what day of the week is this date?
Enrichment	Add new external information—e.g., is this day a public holiday?
Encoding	Present the same information differently—e.g., day of the week or weekday versus weekend.
Combination	Link features together—e.g., the size of the backlog might need to be weighted by the complexity of the different items in it.

For instance, in trying to estimate the potential duration of a business process given the current backlog, if one of the inputs is a date, it is pretty common to derive the corresponding day of the week or how far ahead the next public holiday is from that date. If the business serves multiple locations that observe different business calendars, that information may also be important.

Another example, to follow up on the house pricing scenario from the previous section, would be using average income and population density, which ideally allows the model to better generalize and train on more diverse data than trying to segment by area (i.e., zip code).

Feature Engineering Techniques

A whole market exists for such complementary data that extends far beyond the open data that public institutions and companies share. Some services provide direct enrichment that can save a lot of time and effort.

There are, however, many cases when information that data scientists need for their models is not available. In this case, there are techniques like impact coding, whereby data scientists replace a modality by the average value of the target for that modality, thus allowing the model to benefit from data in a similar range (at the cost of some information loss).

Ultimately, most ML algorithms require a table of numbers as input, each row representing a sample, and all samples coming from the same dataset. When the input data is not tabular, data scientists can use other tricks to transform it.

The most common one is *one-hot encoding*. For example, a feature that can take three values (e.g., Raspberry, Blueberry, and Strawberry) is transformed into three features that can take only two values—yes or no (e.g., Raspberry yes/no, Blueberry yes/no, Strawberry yes/no).

Text or image inputs, on the other hand, require more complex engineering. Deep learning has recently revolutionized this field by providing models that transform images and text into tables of numbers that are usable by ML algorithms. These tables are called *embeddings*, and they allow data scientists to perform transfer learning because they can be used in domains on which they were not trained.

Transfer Learning

Transfer learning is the technique of using information gained from solving one problem in solving a different problem. Transfer learning can be used to significantly accelerate learning of second or subsequent tasks, and it is very popular in deep learning, where the resources needed to train models can be enormous.

For example, even if a particular deep learning model was trained on images that did not contain any forks, it may give a useful embedding to be used by a model that is trained to detect them, because a fork is an object, and that model was trained to detect similar human-made objects.

How Feature Selection Impacts MLOps Strategy

When it comes to feature creation and selection, the question of how much and when to stop comes up regularly. Adding more features may produce a more accurate model, achieve more fairness when splitting into more precise groups, or compensate for some other useful missing information. However, it also comes with downsides, all of which can have a significant impact on MLOps strategies down the line:

- The model can become more and more expensive to compute.
- More features require more inputs and more maintenance down the line.
- More features mean a loss of some stability.
- The sheer number of features can raise privacy concerns.

Automated feature selection can help by using heuristics to estimate how critical some features will be for the predictive performance of the model. For instance, one can look at the correlation with the target variable or quickly train a simple model on a representative subset of the data and then look at which features are the strongest predictors.

Which inputs to use, how to encode them, how they interact or interfere with each other—such decisions require a certain understanding of the inner workings of the ML algorithm. The good news is that some of this can be partly automated, e.g., by using tools such as Auto-sklearn or AutoML applications that cross-reference features against a given target to estimate which features, derivatives, or combinations are likely to yield the best results, leaving out all the features that would probably not make that much of a difference.

Other choices still require human intervention, such as deciding whether to try to collect additional information that might improve the model. Spending time to build business-friendly features will often improve the final performance and ease the adoption by end users, as model explanations are likely to be simpler. It can also reduce modeling debt, allowing data scientists to understand the main prediction drivers and ensure that they are robust. Of course, there are trade-offs to consider between the cost of time spent to understand the model and the expected value, as well as risks associated with the model's use.

Feature Stores

Feature factories, or feature stores, are repositories of different features associated with business entities that are created and stored in a central location for easier reuse. They usually combine an offline part (slower, but potentially more powerful) and an online part (quicker and more useful for real-time needs), making sure they remain consistent with each other.

Given how time-consuming feature engineering is for data scientists, feature stores have huge potential to free up their time for even more valuable tasks. Machine learning is still often the "high-interest credit card of technical debt" (*https://oreil.ly/IYXUi*). Reversing this will require huge efficiency gains in the data-to-model-to-production process and in the MLOps process, and feature stores are one way to get there.

The bottom line is that when building models, the process of engineering and selecting features, like many other ML model components, is a delicate balance between considering MLOps components and performance.

Experimentation

Experimentation takes place throughout the entire model development process, and usually every important decision or assumption comes with at least some experiment or previous research to justify it. Experimentation can take many shapes, from building full-fledged predictive ML models to doing statistical tests or charting data. Goals of experimentation include:

- Assessing how useful or how good of a model can be built given the elements outlined in Table 4-1. (The next section will cover model evaluation and comparison in more detail.)

- Finding the best modeling parameters (algorithms, hyperparameters, feature preprocessing, etc.).

- Tuning the bias/variance trade-off for a given training cost to fit that definition of "best."

- Finding a balance between model improvement and improved computation costs. (Since there's always room for improvement, how good is good enough?)

Bias and Variance

A high bias model (also known as *underfitting*) fails to discover some of the rules that could have been learned from the training data, possibly because of reductive assumptions making the model overly simplistic.

A high variance model (or *overfitting*) sees patterns in noise and seeks to predict every single variation, resulting in a complex model that does not generalize well beyond its training data.

When experimenting, data scientists need to be able to quickly iterate through all the possibilities for each of the model building blocks outlined in Table 4-1. Fortunately, there are tools to do all of this semiautomatically, where you only need to define what should be tested (the space of possibilities) depending on prior knowledge (what makes sense) and the constraints (e.g., computation, budget).

Some tools allow for even more automation, for instance by offering stratified model training. For example, say the business wants to predict customer demand for products to optimize inventory, but behavior varies a lot from one store to the next. Stratified modeling consists of training one model per store that can be better optimized for each store rather than a model that tries to predict in all stores.

Trying all combinations of every possible hyperparameter, feature handling, etc., quickly becomes untraceable. Therefore, it is useful to define a time and/or computation budget for experiments as well as an acceptability threshold for usefulness of the model (more on that notion in the next section).

Notably, all or part of this process may need to be repeated every time anything in the situation changes (including whenever the data and/or problem constraints change significantly; see "Drift Detection in Practice" on page 92). Ultimately, this means that all experiments that informed the final decisions data scientists made to arrive at the model as well as all the assumptions and conclusions along the way may need to be rerun and reexamined.

Fortunately, more and more data science and machine learning platforms allow for automating these workflows not only on the first run, but also to preserve all the processing operations for repeatability. Some also allow for the use of version control and experimental branch spin-off to test theories and then merge, discard, or keep them (see "Version Management and Reproducibility" on page 56).

Evaluating and Comparing Models

George E. P. Box, a twentieth century British statistician, once said that all models are wrong, but some are useful. In other words, a model should not aim to be perfect, but it should pass the bar of "good enough to be useful" while keeping an eye on the uncanny valley—typically a model that *looks* like it's doing a good job but does a bad (or catastrophic) job for a specific subset of cases (say, an underrepresented population).

With this in mind, it's important to evaluate a model in context and have some ability to compare it to what existed before the model—whether a previous model or a rules-based process—to get an idea of what the outcome would be if the current model or decision process were replaced by the new one.

A model with an absolute performance that could technically be considered disappointing can still possibly enhance an existing situation. For instance, having a slightly more accurate forecast of demand for a certain product or service may result in huge cost-savings.

Conversely, a model that gets a perfect score is suspicious, as most problems have noise in the data that's at least somewhat hard to predict. A perfect or nearly-perfect score may be a sign that there is a leak in the data (i.e., that the target to be predicted is also in the input data or that an input feature is very correlated to the target but, practically, available only once the target is known) or that the model overfits the training data and will not generalize well.

Choosing Evaluation Metrics

Choosing the proper metric by which to evaluate and compare different models for a given problem can lead to very different models (think of the cobra effect mentioned in Table 4-1). A simple example: accuracy is often used for automated classification problems but is rarely the best fit when the classes are unbalanced (i.e., when one of the outcomes is very unlikely compared to the other). In a binary classification problem where the positive class (i.e., the one that is interesting to predict because its prediction triggers an action) is rare, say 5% of occurrences, a model that constantly predicts the negative class is therefore 95% accurate, while also utterly useless.

Unfortunately, there is no one-size-fits-all metric. You need to pick one that matches the problem at hand, which means understanding the limits and trade-offs of the metric (the mathematics side) and their impact on the optimization of the model (the business side).

To get an idea of how well a model will generalize, that metric should be evaluated on a part of the data that was not used for the model's training (a holdout dataset), a method called *cross-testing*. There can be multiple steps where some data is held for evaluation and the rest is used for training or optimizing, such as metric evaluation or hyperparameter optimization. There are different strategies as well, not necessarily just a simple split. In *k*-fold cross-validation, for example, data scientists rotate the parts that they hold out to evaluate and train multiple times. This multiplies the training time but gives an idea of the stability of the metric.

With a simple split, the holdout dataset can consist of the most recent records instead of randomly chosen ones. Indeed, as models are usually used for future predictions, it is likely that assessing them as if they were used for prediction on the most recent data leads to more realistic estimations. In addition, it allows one to assess whether the data drifted between the training and the holdout dataset (see "Drift Detection in Practice" on page 92 for more details).

As an example, Figure 4-2 shows a scheme in which a test dataset is a holdout (in gray) in order to perform the evaluation. The remaining data is split into three parts to find the best hyperparameter combination by training the model three times with a given combination on each of the blue datasets, and validating its performance on their respective green datasets. The gray dataset is used only once with the best hyperparameter combination, while the other datasets are used with all of them.

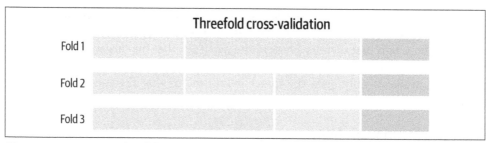

Figure 4-2. An example of dataset split for model evaluation

Oftentimes, data scientists want to periodically retrain models with the same algorithms, hyperparameters, features, etc., but on more recent data. Naturally, the next step is to compare the two models and see how the new version fares. But it's also important to make sure all previous assumptions still hold: that the problem hasn't fundamentally shifted, that the modeling choices made previously still fit the data, etc. This is more specifically part of performance and drift monitoring (find more details on this in Chapter 7).

Cross-Checking Model Behavior

Beyond the raw metrics, when evaluating a model, it's critical to understand how it will behave. Depending on the impact of the model's predictions, decisions, or classifications, a more or less deep understanding may be required. For example, data scientists should take reasonable steps (with respect to that impact) to ensure that the model is not actively harmful: a model that would predict that *all* patients need to be checked by a doctor may score high in terms of raw prevention, but not so much on realistic resource allocation.

Examples of these reasonable steps include:

- Cross-checking different metrics (and not only the ones on which the model was initially optimized)
- Checking how the model reacts to different inputs—e.g., plot the average prediction (or probability for classification models) for different values of some inputs and see whether there are oddities or extreme variability
- Splitting one particular dimension and checking the difference in behavior and metrics across different subpopulations—e.g., is the error rate the same for males and females?

These kinds of global analyses should not be understood as causality, just as correlation. They do not necessarily imply a specific causal relationship between some variables and an outcome; they merely show how the *model* sees that relationship. In other words, the model should be used with care for what-if analysis. If one feature value is changed, the model prediction is likely to be wrong if the new feature value has never been seen in the training dataset or if it has never been seen in combination with the values of the other features in this dataset.

When comparing models, those different aspects should be accessible to data scientists, who need to be able to go deeper than a single metric. That means the full environment (interactive tooling, data, etc.) needs to be available for all models, ideally allowing for comparison from all angles and between all components. For example, for drift, the comparison might use the same settings but different data, while for modeling performance, it might use the same data but different settings.

Impact of Responsible AI on Modeling

Depending on the situation (and sometimes depending on the industry or sector of the business), on top of a general understanding of model behavior, data scientists may also need models' individual predictions to be explainable, including having an idea of what specific features pushed the prediction one way or the other. Sometimes predictions may be very different for a specific record than on average. Popular methods to compute individual prediction explanations include Shapley value (the average marginal contribution of a feature value across all possible coalitions) and individual conditional expectation (ICE) computations, which show the dependence between the target functions and features of interest.

For example, the measured level of a specific hormone could generally push a model to predict someone has a health issue, but for a pregnant woman, that level makes the model infer she is at no such risk. Some legal frameworks mandate some kind of explainability for decisions made by a model that have consequences on humans, like recommending a loan to be denied. "Element 2: Bias" on page 114 discusses this topic in detail.

Note that the notion of explainability has several dimensions. In particular, deep learning networks are sometimes called *black-box* models because of their complexity (though when reading the model coefficients, a model is fully specified, and it is usually a conceptually remarkably simple formula, but a very large formula that becomes impossible to intuitively apprehend). Conversely, global and local explanation tools—such as partial dependence plots or Shapley value computations—give some insights but arguably do not make the model intuitive. To actually communicate a rigorous and intuitive understanding of what exactly the model is doing, limiting the model complexity is required.

Fairness requirements can also have dimensioning constraints on model development. Consider this theoretical example to better understand what is at stake when it comes to bias: a US-based organization regularly hires people who do the same types of jobs. Data scientists could train a model to predict the workers' performance according to various characteristics, and people would then be hired based on the probability that they would be high-performing workers.

Though this seems like a simple problem, unfortunately, it's fraught with pitfalls. To make this problem completely hypothetical and to detach it from the complexities and problems of the real world, let's say everyone in the working population belongs to one of two groups: Weequay or Togruta.

For this hypothetical example, let's claim that a far larger population of Weequay attend university. Off the bat, there would be an initial bias in favor of Weequay (amplified by the fact they would have been able to develop their skills through years of experience).

As a result, there would not only be more Weequay than Togruta in the pool of applicants, but Weequay applicants would tend to be more qualified. The employer has to hire 10 people during the month to come. What should it do?

- As an equal opportunity employer, it should ensure the fairness of its recruitment process as it controls it. That means in mathematical terms, for each applicant and all things being equal, being hired (or not) should not depend on their group affiliation (in this case, Weequay or Togruta). However, this results in bias in and of itself, as Weequay are more qualified. Note that "all things being equal" can be interpreted in various ways, but the usual interpretation is that the organization is likely not considered accountable for processes it does not control.

- The employer may also have to avoid disparate impact, that is, practices in employment that adversely affect one group of people of a protected characteristic more than another. Disparate impact is assessed on subpopulations and not on individuals; practically, it assesses whether proportionally speaking, the company has hired as many Weequay as Togruta. Once again, the target proportions may be those of the applicants or those of the general population, though the former is more likely, as again, the organization can't be accountable for biases in processes out of its control.

The two objectives are mutually exclusive. In this scenario, equal opportunity would lead to hiring 60% (or more) Weequay and 40% (or fewer) Togruta. As a result, the process has a disparate impact on the two populations, because the hiring rates are different.

Conversely, if the process is corrected so that 40% of people hired are Togruta to avoid disparate impact, it means that some rejected Weequay applicants will have been predicted as more qualified than some accepted Togruta applicants (contradicting the equal opportunity assertion).

There needs to be a trade-off—the law sometimes referred to as the 80% rule. In this example, it would mean that the hiring rate of Togruta should be equal to or larger than 80% of the hiring rate of Weequay. In this example, it means that it would be OK to hire up to 65% Weequay.

The point here is that defining these objectives cannot be a decision made by data scientists alone. But even once the objectives are defined, the implementation itself may also be problematic:

- Without any indications, data scientists naturally try to build equal opportunity models because they correspond to models of the world as it is. Most of the tools data scientists employ also try to achieve this because it is the most mathematically sound option. Yet some ways to achieve this goal may be unlawful. For example, the data scientist may choose to implement two independent models: one for Weequay and one for Togruta. This could be a reasonable way to address the biases induced by a training dataset in which Weequay are overrepresented, but it would induce a disparate treatment of the two that could be considered discriminatory.

- To let data scientists use their tools in the way they were designed (i.e., to model the world as it is), they may decide to post-process the predictions so that they fit with the organization's vision of the world as it should be. The simplest way of doing this is to choose a higher threshold for Weequay than for Togruta. The gap between them will adjust the trade-off between "equal opportunity" and "equal impact"; however, it may still be considered discriminatory because of the disparate treatment.

Data scientists are unlikely to be able to sort this problem out alone (see "Key Elements of Responsible AI" on page 113 for a broader view on the subject). This simple example illustrates the complexity of the subject, which may be even more complex given that there may be many protected attributes, and the fact that bias is as much a business question as a technical question.

Consequently, the solution heavily depends on the context. For instance, this example of Weequay and Togruta is representative of processes that give access to privileges. The situation is different if the process has negative impacts on the user (like fraud prediction that leads to transaction rejection) or is neutral (like disease prediction).

Version Management and Reproducibility

Discussing the evaluation and comparison of models (for fairness as discussed immediately before, but also a host of other factors) necessarily brings up the idea of version control and the reproducibility of different model versions. With data scientists building, testing, and iterating on several versions of models, they need to be able to keep all the versions straight.

Version management and reproducibility address two different needs:

- During the experimentation phase, data scientists may find themselves going back and forth on different decisions, trying out different combinations, and reverting when they don't produce the desired results. That means having the ability to go back to different "branches" of the experiments—for example, restoring a previous state of a project when the experimentation process led to a dead end.
- Data scientists or others (auditors, managers, etc.) may need to be able to replay the computations that led to model deployment for an audit team several years after the experimentation was first done.

Versioning has arguably been somewhat solved when everything is code-based, with source version control technology. Modern data processing platforms typically offer similar capabilities for data transformation pipelines, model configuration, etc. Merging several parts is, of course, less straightforward than merging code that diverged, but the basic need is to be able to go back to some specific experiment, if only to be able to copy its settings to replicate them in another branch.

Another very important property of a model is reproducibility. After a lot of experiments and tweaking, data scientists may arrive at a model that fits the bill. But after that, operationalization necessitates model reproduction not only in another environment, but also possibly from a different starting point. Repeatability also makes debugging much easier (sometimes even simply possible). To this end, all facets of the model need to be documented and reusable, including:

Assumptions
When a data scientist makes decisions and assumptions about the problem at hand, its scope, the data, etc., they should all be explicit and logged so that they can be checked against any new information down the line.

Randomness
A lot of ML algorithms and processes, such as sampling, make use of pseudo-random numbers. Being able to precisely reproduce an experiment, such as for debugging, means to have control over that pseudo-randomness, most often by controlling the "seed" of the generator (i.e., the same generator initialized with the same seed would yield the same sequence of pseudo-random numbers).

Data
To get repeatability, the same data must be available. This can sometimes be tricky because the storage capacity required to version data can be prohibitive depending on the rate of update and quantity. Also, branching on data does not yet have as rich an ecosystem of tools as branching on code.

Settings
This one is a given: all processing that has been done must be reproducible with the same settings.

Results
While developers use merging tools to compare and merge different text file versions, data scientists need to be able to compare in-depth analysis of models (from confusion matrices to partial dependence plots) to obtain models that satisfy the requirements.

Implementation
Ever-so-slightly different implementations of the same model can actually yield different models, enough to change the predictions on some close calls. And the more sophisticated the model, the higher the chances that these discrepancies happen. On the other hand, scoring a dataset in bulk with a model comes with different constraints than scoring a single record live in an API, so different implementations may sometimes be warranted for the same model. But when

debugging and comparing, data scientists need to keep the possible differences in mind.

Environment

Given all the steps covered in this chapter, it's clear that a model is not just its algorithm and parameters. From the data preparation to the scoring implementation, including feature selection, feature encoding, enrichment, etc., the environment in which several of those steps run may be more or less implicitly tied to the results. For instance, a slightly different version of a Python package involved in one step may change the results in ways that can be hard to predict. Preferably, data scientists should make sure that the runtime environment is also repeatable. Given the pace at which ML is evolving, this might require techniques that freeze the computation environments.

Fortunately, part of the underlying documentation tasks associated with versioning and reproducibility can be automated, and the use of an integrated platform for design and deployment can greatly decrease the reproducibility costs by ensuring structured information transfer.

Clearly, while maybe not the sexiest part of model development, version management and reproducibility are critical to building machine learning efforts in real-world organizational settings where governance—including audits—matters.

Closing Thoughts

Model development is one of the most critical and consequential steps of MLOps. The many technical questions that are necessarily answered during this phase have big repercussions on all aspects of the MLOps process throughout the life of the models. Therefore, exposure, transparency, and collaboration are crucial to long-term success.

The model development stage is also the one that has been practiced the most by profiles like data scientists and, in the pre-MLOps world, often represents the whole ML effort, yielding a model that will then be used as is (with all its consequences and limitations).

CHAPTER 5

Preparing for Production

Joachim Zentici

Confirming that something works in the laboratory has never been a sure sign it will work well in the real world, and machine learning models are no different. Not only is the production environment typically very different from the development environment, but the commercial risks associated with models in production are much greater. It is important that the complexities of the transition to production are understood and tested and that the potential risks have been adequately mitigated.

This chapter explores the steps required to prepare for production (highlighted in the context of the entire life cycle in Figure 5-1). The goal is to illustrate, by extension, the elements that must be considered for robust MLOps systems.

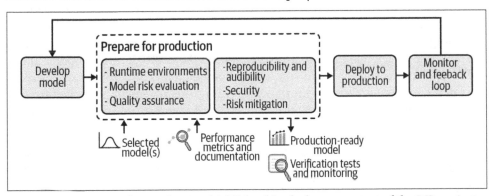

Figure 5-1. Preparing for production highlighted in the larger context of the ML project life cycle

Runtime Environments

The first step in sending a model to production is making sure it's technically possible. As discussed in Chapter 3, ideal MLOps systems favor rapid, automated deployment over labor-intensive processes, and runtime environments can have a big effect on which approach prevails.

Production environments take a wide variety of forms: custom-built services, data science platforms, dedicated services like TensorFlow Serving, low-level infrastructure like Kubernetes clusters, JVMs on embedded systems, etc. To make things even more complex, consider that in some organizations, multiple heterogeneous production environments coexist.

Ideally, models running in the development environment would be validated and sent as is to production; this minimizes the amount of adaptation work and improves the chances that the model in production will behave as it did in development. Unfortunately, this ideal scenario is not always possible, and it's not unheard of that teams finish a long-term project only to realize it can't be put in production.

Adaptation from Development to Production Environments

In terms of adaptation work, on one end of the spectrum, the development and production platforms are from the same vendor or are otherwise interoperable, and the dev model can run without any modification in production. In this case, the technical steps required to push the model into production are reduced to a few clicks or commands, and all efforts can be focused on validation.

On the other end of the spectrum, there are cases where the model needs to be reimplemented from scratch—possibly by another team, and possibly in another programming language. Given the resources and time required, there are few cases today where this approach makes sense. However, it's still the reality in many organizations and is often a consequence of the lack of appropriate tooling and processes. The reality is that handing over a model for another team to reimplement and adapt for the production environment means that model won't reach production for months (maybe years), if at all.

Between these two extreme cases, there can be a number of transformations performed on the model or the interactions with its environment to make it compatible with production. In all cases, it is crucial to perform validation in an environment that mimics production as closely as possible, rather than in the development environment.

Tooling considerations

The format required to send to production should be considered early, as it may have a large impact on the model itself and the quantity of work required to productionalize it. For example, when a model is developed using scikit-learn (Python) and production is a Java-based environment that expects PMML or ONNX as input, conversion is obviously required.

In this case, teams should set up tooling while developing the model, ideally before the first version of the model is finished or even started. Failure to create this pipeline up front would block the validation process (and, of course, final validation should not be performed on the scikit-learn model, as it's not the one that will be put into production).

Performance considerations

Another common reason conversion may be required is for performance. For example, a Python model will typically have higher latency for scoring a single record than its equivalent converted to C++. The resulting model will likely be dozens of times faster (although obviously it depends on many factors, and the result can also be a model that is dozens of times slower).

Performance also comes into play when the production model must run on a low-power device. In the specific case of deep neural networks, for example, trained models can become extremely large with billions or hundreds of billions of parameters. Running them on small devices is simply impossible, and running them on standard servers can be slow and expensive.

For these models, an optimized runtime is not enough. To obtain better performance, the model definition must be optimized. One solution is to use compression techniques:

- With quantization, the model can be trained using 32-bit floating-point numbers and used for inference at a lower precision so that the model requires less memory and is faster while accuracy is mostly preserved.

- With pruning, one simply removes weights (or even entire layers) from the neural network. This is a rather radical approach, but some methods allow for the preservation of accuracy.

- With distillation, a smaller "student" network is trained to mimic a bigger, more powerful network. Done appropriately, this can lead to better models (as compared to trying to train the smaller network directly from the data).

These methods are efficient if the initial model is trained in a way that reduces information loss while performing them, so these operations are not simply conversions of the trained model post hoc, but rather orient the way the model is trained. These methods are still very recent and quite advanced but already commonly used in natural language processing (NLP) pretrained models.

Data Access Before Validation and Launch to Production

Another technical aspect that needs to be addressed before validation and launch to production is data access. For example, a model evaluating apartment prices may use the average market price in a zip code area; however, the user or the system requesting the scoring will probably not provide this average and would most likely provide simply the zip code, meaning a lookup is necessary to fetch the value of the average.

In some cases, data can be frozen and bundled with the model. But when this is not possible (e.g., if the dataset is too large or the enrichment data needs to always be up to date), the production environment should access a database and thus have the appropriate network connectivity, libraries, or drivers required to communicate with the data storage installed, and authentication credentials stored in some form of production configuration.

Managing this setup and configuration can be quite complex in practice since, again, it requires appropriate tooling and collaboration (in particular to scale to more than a few dozen models). When using external data access, model validation in situations that closely match production is even more critical as technical connectivity is a common source of production malfunction.

Final Thoughts on Runtime Environments

Training a model is usually the most impressive computation, requiring a high level of software sophistication, massive data volumes, and high-end machines with powerful GPUs. But in the whole life cycle of a model, there is a good chance that most of the compute is spent at inference time (even if this computation is orders of magnitude simpler and faster). This is because a model is trained once and can be used billions of times for inference.

Scaling inference on complex models can be expensive and have significant energy and environmental impact. Lowering the complexity of models or compressing extremely complex models can lower the infrastructure cost of operating machine learning models.

It's important to remember that not all applications require deep learning, and in fact, not all applications require machine learning at all. A valuable practice to control complexity in production is to develop complex models only to provide a baseline for what seems achievable. What goes into production can then be a much simpler model, with the advantages of lowering the operating risk, increasing computational performance, and lowering power consumption. If the simple model is close enough to the high complexity baseline, then it can be a much more desirable solution for production.

Model Risk Evaluation

Before exploring how validation should be done in an ideal MLOps system, it's important to consider the purpose of validation. As discussed in Chapter 4, models attempt to mimic reality, but they are imperfect; their implementation can have bugs, as can the environment they are executing in. The indirect, real-world impact a model in production can have is never certain, and the malfunctioning of a seemingly insignificant cog can have tremendous consequences in a complex system.

The Purpose of Model Validation

It is, to some extent, possible (not to mention absolutely necessary) to anticipate the risks of models in production and thus design and validate so as to minimize these risks. As organizations become more and more complex, it is essential to understand that involuntary malfunctions or malicious attacks are potentially threatening in most uses of machine learning in the enterprise, not only in financial or safety-related applications.

Before putting a model in production (and in fact constantly from the beginning of the machine learning project), teams should ask the uncomfortable questions:

- What if the model acts in the worst imaginable way?
- What if a user manages to extract the training data or the internal logic of the model?
- What are the financial, business, legal, safety, and reputational risks?

For high-risk applications, it is essential that the whole team (and in particular the engineers in charge of validation) be fully aware of these risks so that they can design the validation process appropriately and apply the strictness and complexity appropriate for the magnitude of the risks.

In many ways, machine learning risk management covers model risk management practices that are well established in many industries, such as banking and insurance. However, machine learning introduces new types of risks and liabilities, and as data science gets democratized, it involves many new organizations or teams that have no experience with more traditional model risk management.

The Origins of ML Model Risk

The magnitude of risk ML models can bring is hard to model for mathematical reasons, but also because the materialization of risks arises through real-world consequences. The ML metrics, and in particular the cost matrix, allow teams to evaluate the average cost of operating a model in its "nominal" case, meaning on its cross-validation data, compared to operating a perfect magical model.

But while computing this expected cost can be very important, a wide range of things can go wrong well beyond expected cost. In some applications, the risk can be a financially unbounded liability, a safety issue for individuals, or an existential threat for the organization. ML model risk originates essentially from:

- Bugs, errors in designing, training, or evaluating the model (including data prep)
- Bugs in the runtime framework, bugs in the model post-processing/conversion, or hidden incompatibilities between the model and its runtime
- Low quality of training data
- High difference between production data and training data
- Expected error rates, but with failures that have higher consequences than expected
- Misuse of the model or misinterpretation of its outputs
- Adversarial attacks
- Legal risk originating in particular from copyright infringement or liability for the model output
- Reputational risk due to bias, unethical use of machine learning, etc.

The probability of materialization of the risk and its magnitude can be amplified by:

- Broad use of the model
- A rapidly changing environment
- Complex interactions between models

The following sections provide more details on these threats and how to mitigate them, which should ultimately be the goal of any MLOps system the organization puts in place.

Quality Assurance for Machine Learning

Software engineering has developed a mature set of tools and methodologies for quality assurance (QA), but the equivalent for data and models is still in its infancy, which makes it challenging to incorporate into MLOps processes. The statistical methods as well as documentation best practices are well known, but implementing them at scale is not common.

Though it's being covered as a part of this chapter on preparing for production, to be clear, QA for machine learning does not occur only at the final validation stage; rather, it should accompany all stages of model development. Its purpose is to ensure compliance with processes as well as ML and computational performance requirements, with a level of detail that is proportionate to the level of risk.

In the case where the people in charge of validation are not the ones who developed the model, it is essential that they have enough training in machine learning and understand the risks so that they can design appropriate validation or detect breaches in the validation proposed by the development team. It is also essential that the organization's structure and culture give them the authority to appropriately report issues and contribute to continuous improvement or block passage to production if the level of risk justifies it.

Robust MLOps practices dictate that performing QA before sending to production is not only about technical validation. It is also the occasion to create documentation and validate the model against organizational guidelines. In particular, this means the origin of all input datasets, pretrained models, or other assets should be known, as they could be subject to regulations or copyrights. For this reason (and for computer security reasons in particular), some organizations choose to allow only whitelisted dependencies. While this can significantly impact the ability of data scientists to innovate quickly, though the list of dependencies can be reported and checked partly automatically, it can also provide additional safety.

Key Testing Considerations

Obviously, model testing will consist of applying the model to carefully curated data and validating measurements against requirements. How the data is selected or generated as well as how much data is required is crucial, but it will depend on the problem tackled by the model.

There are some scenarios in which the test data should not always match "real-world" data. For example, it can be a good idea to prepare a certain number of scenarios, and while some of them should match realistic situations, other data should be specifically generated in ways that could be problematic (e.g., extreme values, missing values).

Metrics must be collected on both statistical (accuracy, precision, recall, etc.) as well as computational (average latency, 95th latency percentile, etc.) aspects, and the test scenarios should fail if some assumptions on them are not verified. For example, the test should fail if the accuracy of the model falls below 90%, the average inference time goes above 100 milliseconds, or more than 5% of inferences take more than 200 milliseconds. These assumptions can also be called *expectations*, *checks*, or *assertions*, as in traditional software engineering.

Statistical tests on results can also be performed but are typically used for subpopulations. It is also important to be able to compare the model with its previous version. It can allow putting in place a champion/challenger approach (described in detail in "Champion/Challenger" on page 100) or checking that a metric does not suddenly drop.

Subpopulation Analysis and Model Fairness

It can be useful to design test scenarios by splitting data into subpopulations based on a "sensitive" variable (that may or may not be used as a feature of the model). This is how fairness (typically between genders) is evaluated.

Virtually all models that apply to people should be analyzed for fairness. Increasingly, failure to assess model fairness will have business, regulatory, and reputational implications for organizations. For details about biases and fairness, refer to "Impact of Responsible AI on Modeling" on page 53 and "Key Elements of Responsible AI" on page 113.

In addition to validating the ML and computational performance metrics, model stability is an important testing property to consider. When changing one feature slightly, one expects small changes in the outcome. While this cannot be always true, it is generally a desirable model property. A very unstable model introduces a lot of complexity and loopholes in addition to delivering a frustrating experience, as the model can feel unreliable even if it has decent performance. There is no single answer to model stability, but generally speaking, simpler models or more regularized ones show better stability.

Reproducibility and Auditability

Reproducibility in MLOps does not have the same meaning as in academia. In the academic world, reproducibility essentially means that the findings of an experiment are described well enough that another competent person can replicate the experiment using the explanations alone, and if the person doesn't make any mistakes, they will arrive at the same conclusion.

In general, reproducibility in MLOps also involves the ability to easily rerun the exact same experiment. It implies that the model comes with detailed documentation, the data used for training and testing, and with an artifact that bundles the implementation of the model plus the full specification of the environment it was run in (see

"Version Management and Reproducibility" on page 56). Reproducibility is essential to prove model findings, but also to debug or build on a previous experiment.

Auditability is related to reproducibility, but it adds some requirements. For a model to be auditable, it must be possible to access the full history of the ML pipeline from a central and reliable storage and to easily fetch metadata on all model versions including:

- The full documentation
- An artifact that allows running the model with its exact initial environment
- Test results, including model explanations and fairness reports
- Detailed model logs and monitoring metadata

Auditability can be an obligation in some highly regulated applications, but it has benefits for all organizations because it can facilitate model debugging, continuous improvement, and keeping track of actions and responsibilities (which is an essential part of governance for responsible applications of ML, as discussed at length in Chapter 8). A full QA toolchain for machine learning—and, thus, MLOps processes—should provide a clear view of model performance with regard to requirements while also facilitating auditability.

Even when MLOps frameworks allow data scientists (or others) to find a model with all its metadata, understanding the model itself can still be challenging (see "Impact of Responsible AI on Modeling" on page 53 for a detailed discussion).

To have a strong practical impact, auditability must allow for intuitive human understanding of all the parts of the system and their version histories. This doesn't change the fact that understanding a machine learning model (even a relatively simple one) requires appropriate training, but depending on the criticality of the application, a wider audience may need to be able to understand the details of the model. As a result, full auditability comes at a cost that should be balanced with the criticality of the model itself.

Machine Learning Security

As a piece of software, a deployed model running in its serving framework can present multiple security issues that range from low-level glitches to social engineering. Machine learning introduces a new range of potential threats where an attacker provides malicious data designed to cause the model to make a mistake.

There are numerous cases of potential attacks. For example, spam filters were an early application of machine learning essentially based on scoring words that were in a dictionary. One way for spam creators to avoid detection was to avoid writing these exact words while still making their message easily understandable by a human reader (e.g., using exotic Unicode characters, voluntarily introducing typos, or using images).

Adversarial Attacks

A more modern but quite analogous example of a machine learning model security issue is an adversarial attack for deep neural networks in which an image modification that can seem minor or even impossible for a human eye to notice can cause the model to drastically change its prediction. The core idea is mathematically relatively simple: since deep learning inference is essentially matrix multiplication, carefully chosen small perturbations to coefficients can cause a large change in the output numbers.

One example of this (*https://arxiv.org/abs/1707.08945*) is that small stickers glued to road signs can confuse an autonomous car's computer vision system, rendering signs invisible or incorrectly classified by the system, while remaining fully visible and understandable to a human being. The more the attacker knows about the system, the more likely they are to find examples that will confuse it.

A human can use reason to find these examples (in particular for simple models). However, for more complex models like deep learning, the attacker will probably need to perform many queries and either use brute force to test as many combinations as possible or use a model to search for problematic examples. The difficulty of countermeasures is increasing with the complexity of models and their availability. Simple models such as logistic regressions are essentially immune, while an open source pretrained deep neural network will basically always be vulnerable, even with advanced, built-in attack detectors (*https://arxiv.org/abs/1705.07263*).

Adversarial attacks don't necessarily happen at inference time. If an attacker can get access to the training data, even partially, then they get control over the system. This kind of attack is traditionally known as a *poisoning attack* in computer security.

One famous example is the Twitter chatbot released by Microsoft in 2016 (*https:// oreil.ly/aBGVq*). Just a few hours after launch, the bot started to generate very offensive tweets. This was caused by the bot adapting to its input; when realizing that some users submitted a large amount of offensive content, the bot started to replicate. In theory, a poisoning attack can occur as a result of an intrusion or even, in a more sophisticated way, through pretrained models. But in practice, one should mostly care about data collected from easily manipulated data sources. Tweets sent to a specific account are a particularly clear example.

Other Vulnerabilities

Some patterns do not exploit machine learning vulnerabilities per se, but they do use the machine learning model in ways that lead to undesirable situations. One example is in credit scoring: for a given amount of money, borrowers with less flexibility tend to choose a longer period to lower the payments, while borrowers who are not concerned about their ability to pay may choose a shorter period to lower the total cost of credit. Salespeople may advise those who do not have a good enough score to shorten their payments. This increases the risk for the borrower *and* the bank and is not a meaningful course of action. Correlation is not causality!

Models can also leak data in many ways. Since the machine learning models can fundamentally be considered a summary of the data they have been trained on, they can leak more or less precise information on the training data, up to the full training set in some cases. Imagine, for example, that a model predicts how much someone is paid using the nearest neighbor algorithm. If one knows the zip code, age, and profession of a certain person registered on the service, it's pretty easy to obtain that person's exact income. There are a wide range of attacks that can extract information from models in this way.

In addition to technical hardening and audit, governance plays a critical role in security. Responsibilities must be assigned clearly and in a way that ensures an appropriate balance between security and capacity of execution. It is also important to put in place feedback mechanisms, and employees and users should have an easy channel to communicate breaches (including, potentially, "bug bounty programs" that reward reporting vulnerabilities). It is also possible, and necessary, to build safety nets around the system to mitigate the risks.

Machine learning security shares many common traits with general computer system security, one of the main ideas being that security is not an additional independent feature of the system; that is, generally you cannot secure a system that is not designed to be secure, and the organization processes must take into account the nature of the threat from the beginning. Strong MLOps processes, including all of the steps in preparing for production described in this chapter, can help make this approach a reality.

Model Risk Mitigation

Generally speaking, as discussed in detail in Chapter 1, the broader the model deployment, the greater the risk. When risk impact is high enough, it is essential to control the deployment of new versions, which is where tightly controlled MLOps processes come into play in particular. Progressive or canary rollouts should be a common practice, with new versions of models being served to a small proportion of the organization or customer base first and slowly increasing that proportion, while monitoring behavior and getting human feedback if appropriate.

Changing Environments

Rapidly changing environments also multiply risk, as mentioned earlier in this chapter. Changes in inputs is a related and also well-identified risk, and Chapter 7 dives into these challenges and how to address them in more detail. But what's important to note is that the speed of change can amplify the risk depending on the application. Changes may be so fast that they have consequences even before the monitoring system sends alerts. That is to say, even with an efficient monitoring system and a procedure to retrain models, the time necessary to remediate may be a critical threat, especially if simply retraining the model on new data is not sufficient and a new model must be developed. During this time, the production systems misbehaving can cause large losses for the organization.

To control this risk, monitoring via MLOps should be reactive enough (typically, alerting on distributions computed every week might not be enough), and the procedure should consider the period necessary for remediation. For example, in addition to retraining or rollout strategies, the procedure may define thresholds that would trigger a degraded mode for the system. A degraded mode may simply consist of a warning message displayed for end users, but could be as drastic as shutting down the dysfunctional system to avoid harm until a stable solution can be deployed.

Less dramatic issues that are frequent enough can also do harm that quickly becomes difficult to control. If the environment changes often, even if remediation never seems urgent, a model can always be slightly off, never operating within its nominal case, and the operating cost can be challenging to evaluate. This can only be detected through dedicated MLOps, including relatively long-term monitoring and reevaluating the cost of operating the model.

In many cases, retraining the model on more data will increasingly improve the model, and this problem will eventually disappear, but this can take time. Before this convergence, a solution might be to use a less complex model that may have a lower evaluated performance and may be more consistent in a frequently changing environment.

Interactions Between Models

Complex interactions between models is probably the most challenging source of risk. This class of issue will be a growing concern as ML models become pervasive, and it's an important potential area of focus for MLOps systems. Obviously, adding models will often add complexity to an organization, but the complexity does not necessarily grow linearly in proportion to the number of models; having two models is more complicated to understand than the sum since there are potential interactions between them.

Moreover, the total complexity is heavily determined by how the interactions with models are designed at a local scale and governed at an organizational scale. Using models in chains (where a model uses inputs from another model) can create significant additional complexity as well as totally unexpected results, whereas using models in independent parallel processing chains, which are each as short and explainable as possible, is a much more sustainable way to design large-scale deployment of machine learning.

First, the absence of obvious interactions between models makes the complexity grow closer to linearly (though note that, in practice, it is rarely the case, as there can always be interactions in the real world even if models are not connected). Also, models used in redundant chains of processing can avoid errors—that is, if a decision is based on several independent chains of processing with methods as different as possible, it can be more robust.

Finally, generally speaking, the more complex the model, the more complex its interactions with other systems may be, as it may have many edge cases, be less stability in some domains, overreact to the changes of an upstream model, or confuse a sensitive downstream model, etc. Here again, we see that model complexity has a cost, and a potentially highly unpredictable one at that.

Model Misbehavior

A number of measures can be implemented to avoid model misbehavior, including examining its inputs and outputs in real time. While training a model, it is possible to characterize its domain of applicability by examining the intervals on which the model was trained and validated. If the value of a feature at inference time is out of bounds, the system can trigger appropriate measures (e.g., rejecting the sample or dispatching a warning message).

Controlling feature-value intervals is a useful and simple technique, but it might be insufficient. For example, when training an algorithm to evaluate car prices, the data may have provided examples of recent light cars and old heavy cars, but no recent heavy cars. The performance of a complex model for these is unpredictable. When the number of features is large, this issue becomes unavoidable due to the curse of dimensionality—i.e., the number of combinations is exponential relative to the number of features.

In these situations, more sophisticated methods can be used, including anomaly detection to identify records where the model is used outside of its application domain. After scoring, the outputs of the model can be examined before confirming the inference. In the case of classification, many algorithms provide certainty scores in addition to their prediction, and a threshold can be fixed to accept an inference output. Note that these certainty scores do not typically translate into probabilities, even if they are named this way in the model.

Conformal prediction is a set of techniques that helps calibrate these scores to obtain an accurate estimation of the probability of correctness. For regression, the value can be checked against a predetermined interval. For example, if the model predicts a car costs $50 or $500,000, you may not want to commit any business on this prediction. The complexity of the implemented techniques should be relevant for the level of risk: a highly complex, highly critical model will require more thorough safeguards.

Closing Thoughts

In practice, preparing models for production starts from the beginning at the development phase; that is to say, the requirements of production deployments, security implications, and risk mitigation aspects should be considered when developing the models. MLOps includes having a clear validation step before sending models to production, and the key ideas to successfully prepare models for productions are:

- Clearly identifying the nature of the risks and their magnitudes
- Understanding model complexity and its impact at multiple levels, including increased latency, increased memory and power consumption, lower ability to interpret inference in production, and a harder-to-control risk
- Providing a simple but clear standard of quality, making sure the team is appropriately trained and the organization structure allows for fast and reliable validation processes
- Automating all the validation that can be automated to ensure it is properly and consistently performed while maintaining the ability to deploy quickly

CHAPTER 6

Deploying to Production

Joachim Zentici

Business leaders view the rapid deployment of new systems into production as key to maximizing business value. But this is only true if deployment can be done smoothly and at low risk (software deployment processes have become more automated and rigorous in recent years to address this inherent conflict). This chapter dives into the concepts and considerations when deploying machine learning models to production that impact—and indeed, drive—the way MLOps deployment processes are built (Figure 6-1 presents this phase in the context of the larger life cycle).

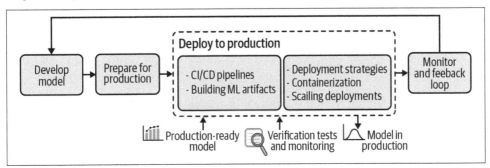

Figure 6-1. Deployment to production highlighted in the larger context of the ML project life cycle

CI/CD Pipelines

CI/CD is a common acronym for continuous integration and continuous delivery (or put more simply, deployment). The two form a modern philosophy of agile software development and a set of practices and tools to release applications more often and faster, while also better controlling quality and risk.

While these ideas are decades old and already used to various extents by software engineers, different people and organizations use certain terms in very different ways. Before digging into how CI/CD applies to machine learning workflows, it is essential to keep in mind that these concepts should be tools to serve the purpose of delivering quality fast, and the first step is always to identify the specific risks present at the organization. In other words, as always, CI/CD methodology should be adapted based on the needs of the team and the nature of the business.

CI/CD concepts apply to traditional software engineering, but they apply just as well to machine learning systems and are a critical part of MLOps strategy. After successfully developing a model, a data scientist should push the code, metadata, and documentation to a central repository and trigger a CI/CD pipeline. An example of such pipeline could be:

1. Build the model
   a. Build the model artifacts
   b. Send the artifacts to long-term storage
   c. Run basic checks (smoke tests/sanity checks)
   d. Generate fairness and explainability reports
2. Deploy to a test environment
   a. Run tests to validate ML performance, computational performance
   b. Validate manually
3. Deploy to production environment
   a. Deploy the model as canary
   b. Fully deploy the model

Many scenarios are possible and depend on the application, the risks from which the system should be protected, and the way the organization chooses to operate. Generally speaking, an incremental approach to building a CI/CD pipeline is preferred: a simple or even naïve workflow on which a team can iterate is often much better than starting with complex infrastructure from scratch.

A starting project does not have the infrastructure requirements of a tech giant, and it can be hard to know up front which challenges deployments will present. There are common tools and best practices, but there is no one-size-fits-all CI/CD methodology. This means the best path forward is starting from a simple (but fully functional) CI/CD workflow and introducing additional or more sophisticated steps along the way as quality or scaling challenges appear.

Building ML Artifacts

The goal of a continuous integration pipeline is to avoid unnecessary effort in merging the work from several contributors as well as to detect bugs or development conflicts as soon as possible. The very first step is using centralized version control systems (unfortunately, working for weeks on code stored only on a laptop is still quite common).

The most common version control system is Git, an open source software initially developed to manage the source code for the Linux kernel. The majority of software engineers across the world already use Git, and it is increasingly being adopted in scientific computing and data science. It allows for maintaining a clear history of changes, safe rollback to a previous version of the code, multiple contributors to work on their own branches of the project before merging to the main branch, etc.

While Git is appropriate for code, it was not designed to store other types of assets common in data science workflows, such as large binary files (for example, trained model weights), or to version the data itself. Data versioning is a more complex topic with numerous solutions, including Git extensions, file formats, databases, etc.

What's in an ML Artifact?

Once the code and data is in a centralized repository, a testable and deployable bundle of the project must be built. These bundles are usually called *artifacts* in the context of CI/CD. Each of the following elements needs to be bundled into an artifact that goes through a testing pipeline and is made available for deployment to production:

- Code for the model and its preprocessing
- Hyperparameters and configuration
- Training and validation data
- Trained model in its runnable form
- An environment including libraries with specific versions, environment variables, etc.
- Documentation
- Code and data for testing scenarios

The Testing Pipeline

As touched on in Chapter 5, the testing pipeline can validate a wide variety of properties of the model contained in the artifact. One of the important operational aspects of testing is that, in addition to verifying compliance with requirements, good tests should make it as easy as possible to diagnose the source issue when they fail.

For that purpose, naming the tests is extremely important, and carefully choosing a number of datasets to validate the model against can be valuable. For example:

- A test on a fixed (not automatically updated) dataset with simple data and not-too-restrictive performance thresholds can be executed first and called "base case." If the test reports show that this test failed, there is a strong possibility that the model is way off, and the cause may be a programming error or a misuse of the model, for example.

- Then, a number of datasets that each have one specific oddity (missing values, extreme values, etc.) could be used with tests appropriately named so that the test report immediately shows the kind of data that is likely to make the model fail. These datasets can represent realistic yet remarkable cases, but it may also be useful to generate synthetic data that is not expected in production. This could possibly protect the model from new situations not yet encountered, but most importantly, this could protect the model from malfunctions in the system querying or from adversarial examples (as discussed in "Machine Learning Security" on page 67).

- Then, an essential part of model validation is testing on recent production data. One or several datasets should be used, extracted from several time windows and named appropriately. This category of tests should be performed and automatically analyzed when the model is already deployed to production. Chapter 7 provides more specific details on how to do that.

Automating these tests as much as possible is essential and, indeed, is a key component of efficient MLOps. A lack of automation or speed wastes time, but, more importantly, it discourages the development team from testing and deploying often, which can delay the discovery of bugs or design choices that make it impossible to deploy to production.

In extreme cases, a development team can hand over a monthslong project to a deployment team that will simply reject it because it does not satisfy requirements for the production infrastructure. Also, less frequent deployments imply larger increments that are harder to manage; when many changes are deployed at once and the system is not behaving in the desired way, isolating the origin of an issue is more time consuming.

The most widespread tool for software engineering continuous integration is Jenkins, a very flexible build system that allows for the building of CI/CD pipelines regardless of the programming language, testing framework, etc. Jenkins can be used in data science to orchestrate CI/CD pipelines, although there are many other options.

Deployment Strategies

To understand the details of a deployment pipeline, it is important to distinguish among concepts often used inconsistently or interchangeably.

Integration
> The process of merging a contribution to a central repository (typically merging a Git feature branch to the main branch) and performing more or less complex tests.

Delivery
> As used in the continuous delivery (CD) part of CI/CD, the process of building a fully packaged and validated version of the model ready to be deployed to production.

Deployment
> The process of running a new model version on a target infrastructure. Fully automated deployment is not always practical or desirable and is a business decision as much as a technical decision, whereas continuous delivery is a tool for the development team to improve productivity and quality as well as measure progress more reliably. Continuous delivery is required for continuous deployment, but it also provides enormous value without.

Release
> In principle, release is yet another step, as deploying a model version (even to the production infrastructure) does not necessarily mean that the production workload is directed to the new version. As we will see, multiple versions of a model can run at the same time on the production infrastructure.

Getting everyone in the MLOps process on the same page about what these concepts mean and how they apply will allow for smoother processes on both the technical and business sides.

Categories of Model Deployment

In addition to different deployment strategies, there are two ways to approach model deployment:

- Batch scoring, where whole datasets are processed using a model, such as in daily scheduled jobs.
- Real-time scoring, where one or a small number of records are scored, such as when an ad is displayed on a website and a user session is scored by models to decide what to display.

There is a continuum between these two approaches, and in fact, in some systems, scoring on one record is technically identical to requesting a batch of one. In both cases, multiple instances of the model can be deployed to increase throughput and potentially lower latency.

Deploying many real-time scoring systems is conceptually simpler since the records to be scored can be dispatched between several machines (e.g., using a load balancer). Batch scoring can also be parallelized, for example by using a parallel processing runtime like Apache Spark, but also by splitting datasets (which is usually called *partitioning* or *sharding*) and scoring the partitions independently. Note that these two concepts of splitting the data and computation can be combined, as they can address different problems.

Considerations When Sending Models to Production

When sending a new model version to production, the first consideration is often to avoid downtime, in particular for real-time scoring. The basic idea is that rather than shutting down the system, upgrading it, and then putting it back online, a new system can be set up next to the stable one, and when it's functional, the workload can be directed to the newly deployed version (and if it remains healthy, the old one is shut down). This deployment strategy is called *blue-green*—or sometimes *red-black*—deployment. There are many variations and frameworks (like Kubernetes) to handle this natively.

Another more advanced solution to mitigate the risk is to have canary releases (also called *canary deployments*). The idea is that the stable version of the model is kept in production, but a certain percentage of the workload is redirected to the new model, and results are monitored. This strategy is usually implemented for real-time scoring, but a version of it could also be considered for batch.

A number of computational performance and statistical tests can be performed to decide whether to fully switch to the new model, potentially in several workload percentage increments. This way, a malfunction would likely impact only a small portion of the workload.

Canary releases apply to production systems, so any malfunction is an incident, but the idea here is to limit the blast radius. Note that scoring queries that are handled by the canary model should be carefully picked, because some issues may go unnoticed otherwise. For example, if the canary model is serving a small percentage of a region or country before the model is fully released globally, it could be the case that (for machine learning or infrastructure reasons) the model does not perform as expected in other regions.

A more robust approach is to pick the portion of users served by the new model at random, but then it is often desirable for user experience to implement an affinity mechanism so that the same user always uses the same version of the model.

Canary testing can be used to carry out A/B testing, which is a process to compare two versions of an application in terms of a business performance metric. The two concepts are related but not the same, as they don't operate at the same level of abstraction. A/B testing can be made possible through a canary release, but it could also be implemented as logic directly coded into a single version of an application. Chapter 7 provides more details on the statistical aspects of setting up A/B testing.

Overall, canary releases are a powerful tool, but they require somewhat advanced tooling to manage the deployment, gather the metrics, specify and run computations on them, display the results, and dispatch and process alerts.

Maintenance in Production

Once a model is released, it must be maintained. At a high level, there are three maintenance measures:

Resource monitoring
Just as for any application running on a server, collecting IT metrics such as CPU, memory, disk, or network usage can be useful to detect and troubleshoot issues.

Health check
To check if the model is indeed online and to analyze its latency, it is common to implement a health check mechanism that simply queries the model at a fixed interval (on the order of one minute) and logs the results.

ML metrics monitoring
This is about analyzing the accuracy of the model and comparing it to another version or detecting when it is going stale. Since it may require heavy computation, this is typically lower frequency, but as always, will depend on the application; it is typically done once a week. Chapter 7 details how to implement this feedback loop.

Finally, when a malfunction is detected, a rollback to a previous version may be necessary. It is critical to have the rollback procedure ready and as automated as possible; testing it regularly can make sure it is indeed functional.

Containerization

As described earlier, managing the versions of a model is much more than just saving its code into a version control system. In particular, it is necessary to provide an exact description of the environment (including, for example, all the Python libraries used as well as their versions, the system dependencies that need to be installed, etc.).

But storing this metadata is not enough. Deploying to production should automatically and reliably rebuild this environment on the target machine. In addition, the target machine will typically run multiple models simultaneously, and two models may have incompatible dependency versions. Finally, several models running on the same machine could compete for resources, and one misbehaving model could hurt the performance of multiple cohosted models.

Containerization technology is increasingly used to tackle these challenges. These tools bundle an application together with all of its related configuration files, libraries, and dependencies that are required for it to run across different operating environments. Unlike virtual machines (VMs), containers do not duplicate the complete operating system; multiple containers share a common operating system and are therefore far more resource efficient.

The most well-known containerization technology is the open source platform Docker. Released in 2014, it has become the de facto standard. It allows an application to be packaged, sent to a server (the Docker host), and run with all its dependencies in isolation from other applications.

Building the basis of a model-serving environment that can accommodate many models, each of which may run multiple copies, may require multiple Docker hosts. When deploying a model, the framework should solve a number of issues:

- Which Docker host(s) should receive the container?
- When a model is deployed in several copies, how can the workload be balanced?
- What happens if the model becomes unresponsive, for example, if the machine hosting it fails? How can that be detected and a container reprovisioned?
- How can a model running on multiple machines be upgraded, with assurances that old and new versions are switched on and off, and that the load balancer is updated with a correct sequence?

Kubernetes, an open source platform that has gained a lot of traction in the past few years and is becoming the standard for container orchestration, greatly simplifies these issues and many others. It provides a powerful declarative API to run applications in a group of Docker hosts, called a Kubernetes *cluster*. The word *declarative* means that rather than trying to express in code the steps to set up, monitor, upgrade, stop, and connect the container (which can be complex and error prone), users specify in a configuration file the desired state, and Kubernetes makes it happen and then maintains it.

For example, users need only specify to Kubernetes "make sure four instances of this container run at all times," and Kubernetes will allocate the hosts, start the containers, monitor them, and start a new instance if one of them fails. Finally, the major cloud providers all provide managed Kubernetes services; users do not even have to install and maintain Kubernetes itself. If an application or a model is packaged as a Docker container, users can directly submit it, and the service will provision the required machines to run one or several instances of the container inside Kubernetes.

Docker with Kubernetes can provide a powerful infrastructure to host applications, including ML models. Leveraging these products greatly simplifies the implementation of the deployment strategies—like blue-green deployments or canary releases—although they are not aware of the nature of the deployed applications and thus can't natively manage the ML performance analysis. Another major advantage of this type of infrastructure is the ability to easily scale the model's deployment.

Scaling Deployments

As ML adoption grows, organizations face two types of growth challenges:

- The ability to use a model in production with high-scale data
- The ability to train larger and larger numbers of models

Handling more data for real-time scoring is made much easier by frameworks such as Kubernetes. Since most of the time trained models are essentially formulas, they can be replicated in the cluster in as many copies as necessary. With the auto-scaling features in Kubernetes, both provisioning new machines and load balancing are fully handled by the framework, and setting up a system with huge scaling capabilities is now relatively simple. The major difficulty can then be to process the large amount of monitoring data; Chapter 7 provides some details on this challenge.

Scalable and Elastic Systems

A computational system is said to be horizontally scalable (or just scalable) if it is possible to incrementally add more computers to expand its processing power. For example, a Kubernetes cluster can be expanded to hundreds of machines. However, if a system includes only one machine, it may be challenging to incrementally upgrade it significantly, and at some point, a migration to a bigger machine or a horizontally scalable system will be required (and may be very expensive and require interruption of service).

An elastic system allows, in addition to being scalable, easy addition and removal of resources to match the compute requirements. For example, a Kubernetes cluster in the cloud can have an auto-scaling capability that automatically adds machines when the cluster usage metrics are high and removes them when they are low. In principle, elastic systems can optimize the usage of resources; they automatically adapt to an increase in usage without the need to permanently provision resources that are rarely required.

For batch scoring, the situation can be more complex. When the volume of data becomes too large, there are essentially two types of strategies to distribute the computation:

- Using a framework that handles distributed computation natively, in particular Spark. Spark is an open source distributed computation framework. It is useful to understand that Spark and Kubernetes do not play similar roles and can be combined. Kubernetes orchestrates containers, but Kubernetes is not aware of what the containers are actually doing; as far as Kubernetes is concerned, they are just containers that run an application on one specific host. (In particular, Kubernetes has no concept of data processing, as it can be used to run any kind of application.) Spark is a computation framework that can split the data and the computation among its nodes. A modern way to use Spark is through Kubernetes. To run a Spark job, the desired number of Spark containers are started by Kubernetes; once they are started, they can communicate to complete the computation, after which the containers are destroyed and the resources are available for other applications, including other Spark jobs that may have different Spark versions or dependencies.

- Another way to distribute batch processing is to partition the data. There are many ways to achieve this, but the general idea is that scoring is typically a row-by-row operation (each row is scored one by one), and the data can be split in some way so that several machines can each read a subset of the data and score a subset of the rows.

In terms of computation, scaling the number of models is somewhat simpler. The key is to add more computing power and to make sure the monitoring infrastructure can handle the workload. But in terms of governance and processes, this is the most challenging situation.

In particular, scaling the number of models means that the CI/CD pipeline must be able to handle large numbers of deployments. As the number of models grows, the need for automation and governance grows, as human verification cannot necessarily be systematic or consistent.

In some applications, it is possible to rely on fully automated continuous deployment if the risks are well controlled by automated validation, canary releases, and automated canary analysis. There can be numerous infrastructure challenges since training, building models, validating on test data, etc., all need to be performed on clusters rather than on a single machine. Also, with a higher number of models, the CI/CD pipeline of each model can vary widely, and if nothing is done, each team will have to develop its own CI/CD pipeline for each model.

This is suboptimal from efficiency and governance perspectives. While some models may need highly specific validation pipelines, most projects can probably use a small number of common patterns. In addition, maintenance is made much more complex as it may become impractical to implement a new systematic validation step, for example, since the pipelines would not necessarily share a common structure and would then be impossible to update safely, even programmatically. Sharing practices and standardized pipelines can help limit complexity. A dedicated tool to manage large numbers of pipelines can also be used; for example, Netflix released Spinnaker, an open source continuous deployment and infrastructure management platform.

Requirements and Challenges

When deploying a model, there are several possible scenarios:

- One model deployed on one server
- One model deployed on multiple servers
- Multiple versions of a model deployed on one server
- Multiple versions of a model deployed on multiple servers
- Multiple versions of multiple models deployed on multiple servers

An effective logging system should be able to generate centralized datasets that can be exploited by the model designer or the ML engineer, usually outside of the production environment. More specifically, it should cover all of the following situations:

- The system can access and retrieve scoring logs from multiple servers, either in a real-time scoring use case or in a batch scoring use case.
- When a model is deployed on multiple servers, the system can handle the mapping and aggregation of all information per model across servers.
- When different versions of a model are deployed, the system can handle the mapping and aggregation of all information per version of the model across servers.

In terms of challenges, for large-scale machine learning applications, the number of raw event logs generated can be an issue if there are no preprocessing steps in place to filter and aggregate data. For real-time scoring use cases, logging streaming data requires setting up a whole new set of tooling that entails a significant engineering effort to maintain. However, in both cases, because the goal of monitoring is usually to estimate aggregate metrics, saving only a subset of the predictions may be acceptable.

Closing Thoughts

Deploying to production is a key component of MLOps, and as dissected in this chapter, having the right processes and tools in place can ensure that it happens quickly. The good news is that many of the elements of success, particularly CI/CD best practices, are not new. Once teams understand how they can be applied to machine learning models, the organization will have a good foundation on which to expand as MLOps scales with the business.

CHAPTER 7

Monitoring and Feedback Loop

Du Phan

When a machine learning model is deployed in production, it can start degrading in quality fast—and without warning—until it's too late (i.e., it's had a potentially negative impact on the business). That's why model monitoring is a crucial step in the ML model life cycle and a critical piece of MLOps (illustrated in Figure 7-1 as a part of the overall life cycle).

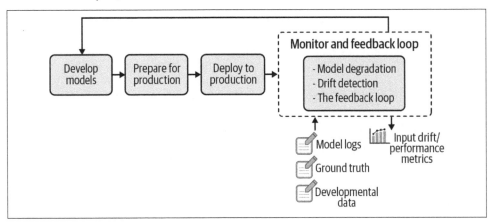

Figure 7-1. Monitoring and feedback loop highlighted in the larger context of the ML project life cycle

Machine learning models need to be monitored at two levels:

- At the resource level, including ensuring the model is running correctly in the production environment. Key questions include: Is the system alive? Are the CPU, RAM, network usage, and disk space as expected? Are requests being processed at the expected rate?

- At the performance level, meaning monitoring the pertinence of the model over time. Key questions include: Is the model still an accurate representation of the pattern of new incoming data? Is it performing as well as it did during the design phase?

The first level is a traditional DevOps topic that has been extensively addressed in the literature (and has been covered in Chapter 6). However, the latter is more complicated. Why? Because how well a model performs is a reflection of the data used to train it; in particular, how representative that training data is of the live request data. As the world is constantly changing, a static model cannot catch up with new patterns that are emerging and evolving without a constant source of new data. While it is possible to detect large deviations on single predictions (see Chapter 5), smaller but still significant deviations have to be detected statistically on datasets of scored rows, with or without ground truth.

Model performance monitoring attempts to track this degradation, and, at an appropriate time, it will also trigger the retraining of the model with more representative data. This chapter delves into detail on how data teams should handle both monitoring and subsequent retraining.

How Often Should Models Be Retrained?

One of the key questions teams have regarding monitoring and retraining is: how often should models be retrained? Unfortunately, there is no easy answer, as this question depends on many factors, including:

The domain
> Models in areas like cybersecurity or real-time trading need to be updated regularly to keep up with the constant changes inherent in these fields. Physical models, like voice recognition, are generally more stable, because the patterns don't often abruptly change. However, even more stable physical models need to adapt to change: what happens to a voice recognition model if the person has a cough and the tone of their voice changes?

The cost
> Organizations need to consider whether the cost of retraining is worth the improvement in performance. For example, if it takes one week to run the whole data pipeline and retrain the model, is it worth a 1% improvement?

The model performance
> In some situations, the model performance is restrained by the limited number of training examples, and thus the decision to retrain hinges on collecting enough new data.

Whatever the domain, the delay to obtain the ground truth is key to defining a lower bound to the retraining period. It is very risky to use a prediction model when there is a possibility that it drifts faster than the lag between prediction time and ground truth obtention time. In this scenario, the model can start giving bad results without any recourse other than to withdraw the model if the drift is too significant. What this means in practice is that it is unlikely a model with a lag of one year is retrained more than a few times a year.

For the same reason, it is unlikely that a model is trained on data collected during a period smaller than this lag. Retraining will not be performed in a shorter period, either. In other words, if the model retraining occurs way more often than the lag, there will be almost no impact of the retraining on the performance of the model.

There are also two organizational bounds to consider when it comes to retraining frequency:

An upper bound
> It is better to perform retraining once every year to ensure that the team in charge has the skills to do it (despite potential turnover—i.e., the possibility that the people retraining the model were not the ones who built it) and that the computing toolchain is still up.

A lower bound
> Take, for example, a model with near-instantaneous feedback, such as a recommendation engine where the user clicks on the product offerings within seconds after the prediction. Advanced deployment schemes will involve shadow testing or A/B testing to make sure that the model performs as anticipated. Because it is a statistical validation, it takes some time to gather the required information. This necessarily sets a lower bound to the retraining period. Even with a simple deployment, the process will probably allow for some human validation or for the possibility of manual rollback, which means it's unlikely that the retraining will occur more than once a day.

Therefore, it is very likely that retraining will be done between once a day and once a year. The simplest solution that consists of retraining the model in the same way and in the same environment it was trained in originally is acceptable. Some critical cases may require retraining in a production environment, even though the initial training was done in a design environment, but the retraining method is usually identical to the training method so that the overall complexity is limited. As always, there is an exception to this rule: online learning.

Online Learning

Sometimes, the use case requires teams to go further than the automation of the existing manual ML pipeline by using dedicated algorithms that can train themselves iteratively. (Standard algorithms, by contrast, are retrained from scratch most of the time, with the exception of deep learning algorithms.)

While conceptually attractive, these algorithms are more costly to set up. The designer has to not only test the performance of the model on a test dataset, but also qualify its behavior when data changes. (The latter is required because it's difficult to mitigate bad learning once the algorithm is deployed, and it's hard to reproduce the behavior when each training recursively relies on the previous one because one needs to replay all the steps to understand the bad behavior). In addition, these algorithms are not stateless: running them twice on the same data will not give the same result because they have learned from the first run.

There is no standard way—similar to cross-validation—to do this process, so the design costs will be higher. Online machine learning is a vivid branch of research with some mature technologies like state-space models, though they require significant skills to be used effectively. Online learning is typically appealing in streaming use cases, though mini batches may be more than enough to handle it.

In any case, some level of model retraining is definitely necessary—it's not a question of if, but of when. Deploying ML models without considering retraining would be like launching an unmanned aircraft from Paris in the exact right direction and hoping it will land safely in New York City without further control.

The good news is that if it was possible to gather enough data to train the model the first time, then most of the solutions for retraining are already available (with the possible exception of cross-trained models that are used in a different context—for example, trained with data from one country but used in another). It is therefore critical for organizations to have a clear idea of deployed models' drift and accuracy by setting up a process that allows for easy monitoring and notifications. An ideal scenario would be a pipeline that automatically triggers checks for degradation of model performance.

It's important to note that the goal of notifications is not necessarily to kick off an automated process of retraining, validation, and deployment. Model performance can change for a variety of reasons, and retraining may not always be the answer. The point is to alert the data scientist of the change; that person can then diagnose the issue and evaluate the next course of action.

It is therefore critical that as part of MLOps and the ML model life cycle, data scientists and their managers and the organization as a whole (which is ultimately the

entity that has to deal with the business consequences of degrading model performances and any subsequent changes) understand model degradation. Practically, every
deployed model should come with monitoring metrics and corresponding warning
thresholds to detect meaningful business performance drops as quickly as possible.
The following sections focus on understanding these metrics to be able to define
them for a particular model.

Understanding Model Degradation

Once a machine learning model is trained and deployed in production, there are two
approaches to monitor its performance degradation: ground truth evaluation and
input drift detection. Understanding the theory behind and limitations of these
approaches is critical to determining the best strategy.

Ground Truth Evaluation

Ground truth retraining requires waiting for the label event. For example, in a fraud
detection model, the ground truth would be whether or not a specific transaction was
actually fraudulent. For a recommendation engine, it would be whether or not the
customer clicked on—or ultimately bought—one of the recommended products.

With the new ground truth collected, the next step is to compute the performance of
the model based on ground truth and compare it with registered metrics in the training phase. When the difference surpasses a threshold, the model can be deemed as
outdated, and it should be retrained.

The metrics to be monitored can be of two varieties:

- Statistical metrics like accuracy, ROC AUC (*https://oreil.ly/tY9Bg*), log loss, etc.
  As the model designer has probably already chosen one of these metrics to pick
  the best model, it is a first-choice candidate for monitoring. For more complex
  models, where the average performance is not enough, it may be necessary to
  look at metrics computed by subpopulations.

- Business metrics, like cost-benefit assessment. For example, the credit scoring
  business has developed its own specific metrics (*https://oreil.ly/SqOr5*).

The main advantage of the first kind of metric is that it is domain agnostic, so the
data scientist likely feels comfortable setting thresholds. So as to have the earliest
meaningful warning, it is even possible to compute *p*-values to assess the probability
that the observed drop is not due to random fluctuations.

> ## A Stats Primer: From Null Hypothesis to *p*-Values
>
> The *null hypothesis* says that there is no relationship between the variables being compared; any results are due to sheer chance.
>
> The *alternative hypothesis* says that the variables being compared are related, and the results are *significant* in supporting the theory being considered, and not due to chance.
>
> The level of statistical significance is often expressed as a *p-value* between 0 and 1. The smaller the *p*-value, the stronger the evidence that one should reject the null hypothesis.

The drawback is that the drop may be statistically significant without having any noticeable impact. Or worse, the cost of retraining and the risk associated with a redeployment may be higher than the expected benefits. Business metrics are far more interesting because they ordinarily have a monetary value, enabling subject matter experts to better handle the cost-benefit trade-off of the retraining decision.

When available, ground truth monitoring is the best solution. However, it may be problematic. There are three main challenges:

- Ground truth is not always immediately, or even imminently, available. For some types of models, teams need to wait months (or longer) for ground truth labels to be available, which can mean significant economic loss if the model is degrading quickly. As said before, deploying a model for which the drift is faster than the lag is risky. However, by definition, drifts are not forecastable, so models with long lags need mitigation measures.

- Ground truth and prediction are decoupled. To compute the performance of the deployed model on new data, it's necessary to be able to match ground truth with the corresponding observation. In many production environments, this is a challenging task because these two pieces of information are generated and stored in different systems and at different timestamps. For low-cost or short-lived models, it might not be worth automated ground truth collection. Note that this is rather short-sighted, because sooner or later, the model will need to be retrained.

- Ground truth is only partially available. In some situations, it is extremely expensive to retrieve the ground truth for all the observations, which means choosing which samples to label and thus inadvertently introducing bias into the system.

For the last challenge, fraud detection presents a clear use case. Given that each transaction needs to be examined manually and the process takes a long time, does it make sense to establish ground truth for only suspect cases (i.e., cases where the model gives a high probability of fraud)? At first glance, the approach seems reasonable; however, a critical mind understands that this creates a feedback loop that will amplify the flaws of the model. Fraud patterns that were never captured by the model (i.e., those that have a low fraud probability according to the model) will never be taken into account in the retraining process.

One solution to this challenge might be to randomly label, establishing a ground truth for just a subsample of transactions in addition to those that were flagged as suspicious. Another solution might be to reweight the biased sample so that its characteristics match the general population more closely. For example, if the system awarded little credit to people with low income, the model should reweight them according to their importance in the applicant, or even in the general, population.

The bottom line is that whatever the mitigation measure, the labeled sample subset must cover all possible future predictions so that the trained model makes good predictions whatever the sample; this will sometimes mean making suboptimal decisions for the sake of checking that the model continues to generalize well.

Once this problem is solved for retraining, the solution (reweighting, random sampling) can be used for monitoring. Input drift detection complements this approach, as it is needed to make sure that ground truth covering new, unexplored domains is made available to retrain the model.

Input Drift Detection

Given the challenges and limitations of ground truth retraining presented in the previous section, a more practical approach might be input drift detection. This section takes a brief but deep dive into the underlying logic behind drift and presents different scenarios that can cause models and data to drift.

Say the goal is to predict the quality of Bordeaux wines using as training data the UCI Wine Quality dataset (*https://oreil.ly/VPx17*), which contains information about red and white variants of the Portuguese wine vinho verde along with a quality score varying between 0 and 10.

The following features are provided for each wine: type, fixed acidity, volatile acidity, citric acid, residual sugar, chlorides, free sulfur dioxide, total sulfur dioxide, density, pH, sulphates, and alcohol rate.

To simplify the modeling problem, say that a good wine is one with a quality score equal to or greater than 7. The goal is thus to build a binary model that predicts this label from the wine's attributes.

To demonstrate data drift, we explicitly split the original dataset into two:

- wine_alcohol_above_11, which contains all wines with an alcohol rate of 11% and above

- wine_alcohol_below_11, which contains all wines with an alcohol rate below 11%

We split wine_alcohol_above_11 to train and score our model, and the second dataset, wine_alcohol_below_11, will be considered as new incoming data that needs to be scored once the model has been deployed.

We have artificially created a big problem: it is very unlikely that the quality of wine is independent from the alcohol level. Worse, the alcohol level is likely to be correlated differently with the other features in the two datasets. As a result, what is learned on one dataset ("if the residual sugar is low and the pH is high, then the probability that the wine is good is high") may be wrong on the other one because, for example, the residual sugar is not important anymore when the alcohol level is high.

Mathematically speaking, the samples of each dataset cannot be assumed to be drawn from the same distribution (i.e., they are not "identically distributed"). Another mathematical property is necessary to ensure that ML algorithms perform as expected: independence. This property is broken if samples are duplicated in the dataset or if it is possible to forecast the "next" sample given the previous one, for example.

Let's assume that despite the obvious problems, we train the algorithm on the first dataset and then deploy it on the second one. The resulting distribution shift is called a drift. It will be called a feature drift if the alcohol level is one of the features used by the ML model (or if the alcohol level is correlated with other features used by the model) and a concept drift if it is not.

Drift Detection in Practice

As explained previously, to be able to react in a timely manner, model behavior should be monitored solely based on the feature values of the incoming data, without waiting for the ground truth to be available.

The logic is that if the data distribution (e.g., mean, standard deviation, correlations between features) diverges between the training and testing phases[1] on one side and the development phase on the other, it is a strong signal that the model's performance won't be the same. It is not the perfect mitigation measure, as retraining on the

---

[1] It is also advisable to assess the drift between the training and the test dataset, especially when the test dataset is posterior to the training dataset. See "Choosing Evaluation Metrics" on page 51 for details.

drifted dataset will not be an option, but it can be part of mitigation measures (e.g., reverting to a simpler model, reweighting).

Example Causes of Data Drift

There are two frequent root causes of data drift:

- Sample selection bias, where the training sample is not representative of the population. For instance, building a model to assess the effectiveness of a discount program will be biased if the best discounts are proposed for the best clients. Selection bias often stems from the data collection pipeline itself. In the wine example, the original dataset sample with alcohol levels above 11% surely does not represent the whole population of wines—this is sample selection at its best. It could have been mitigated if a few samples of wine with an alcohol level above 11% had been kept and reweighted according to the expected proportion in the population of wines to be seen by the deployed model. Note that this task is easier said than done in real life, as the problematic features are often unknown or maybe even not available.

- Non-stationary environment, where training data collected from the source population does not represent the target population. This often happens for time-dependent tasks—such as forecasting use cases—with strong seasonality effects, where learning a model over a given month won't generalize to another month. Back to the wine example: one can imagine a case where the original dataset sample only includes wines from a specific year, which might represent a particularly good (or bad) vintage. A model trained on this data may not generalize to other years.

Input Drift Detection Techniques

After understanding the possible situations that can cause different types of drift, the next logical question is: how can drift be detected? This section presents two common approaches. The choice between them depends on the expected level of interpretability.

Organizations that need proven and explainable methods should prefer univariate statistical tests. If complex drift involving several features simultaneously is expected, or if the data scientists want to reuse what they already know and assuming the organization doesn't dread the black box effect, the domain classifier approach may be a good option, too.

Univariate statistical tests

This method requires applying a statistical test on data from the source distribution and the target distribution for each feature. A warning will be raised when the results of those tests are significant.

The choice of hypothesis tests have been extensively studied in the literature, but the basic approaches rely on these two tests:

- For continuous features, the Kolmogorov-Smirnov test is a nonparametric hypothesis test that is used to check whether two samples come from the same distribution. It measures a distance between the empirical distribution functions.
- For categorical features, the Chi-squared test is a practical choice that checks whether the observed frequencies for a categorical feature in the target data match the expected frequencies seen from the source data.

The main advantage of p-values is that they help detect drift as quickly as possible. The main drawback is that they detect an effect, but they do not quantify the level of the effect (i.e., on large datasets, they detect very small changes, which may be completely without impact). As a result, if development datasets are very large, it is necessary to complement p-values with business-significant metrics. For example, on a sufficiently large dataset, the average age may have significantly drifted from a statistical perspective, but if the drift is only a few months, this is probably an insignificant value for many business use cases.

Domain classifier

In this approach, data scientists train a model that tries to discriminate between the original dataset (input features and, optionally, predicted target) and the development dataset. In other words, they stack the two datasets and train a classifier that aims at predicting the data's origin. The performance of the model (its accuracy, for example) can then be considered as a metric for the drift level.

If this model is successful in its task, and thus has a high drift score, it implies that the data used at training time and the new data can be distinguished, so it's fair to say that the new data has drifted. To gain more insights, in particular to identify the features that are responsible for the drift, one can use the feature importance of the trained model.

Interpretation of results

Both domain classifier and univariate statistical tests point to the importance of features or of the target to explain drift. Drift attributed to the target is important to identify because it often directly impacts the bottom line of the business. (Think, for example, of credit scores: if the scores are lower overall, the number of awarded loans is likely to be lower, and therefore revenue will be lower.) Drift attributed to features is useful to mitigate the impact of drift, as it may hint at the need for:

- Reweighting according to this feature (e.g., if customers above 60 now represent 60% of users but were only 30% in the training set, then double their weight and retrain the model)
- Removing the feature and training a new model without it

In all cases, it is very unlikely that automatic actions exist if drift is detected. It could happen if it is costly to deploy retrained models: the model would be retrained on new data only if performance based on ground truth had dropped or significant drift was detected. In this peculiar case, new data is indeed available to mitigate the drift.

The Feedback Loop

All effective machine learning projects implement a form of data feedback loop; that is, information from the production environment flows back to the model prototyping environment for further improvement.

One can see in Figure 7-2 that data collected in the monitoring and feedback loop is sent to the model development phase (details about this data are covered in Chapter 6). From there, the system analyzes whether the model is working as expected. If it is, no action is required. If the model's performance is degrading, an update will be triggered, either automatically or manually by the data scientist. In practice, as seen at the beginning of this chapter, this usually means either retraining the model with new labeled data or developing a new model with additional features.

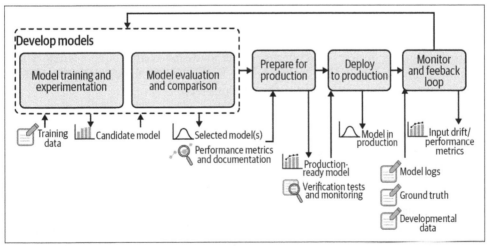

Figure 7-2. Continuous delivery for end-to-end machine learning process

In either case, the goal is to be able to capture the emerging patterns and make sure that the business is not negatively impacted. This infrastructure is comprised of three main components, which in addition to the concepts discussed in the first part of this chapter, are critical to robust MLOps capabilities:

- A logging system that collects data from several production servers
- A model evaluation store that does versioning and evaluation between different model versions
- An online system that does model comparison on production environments, either with the shadow scoring (champion/challenger) setup or with A/B testing

The following sections address each of these components individually, including their purpose, key features, and challenges.

Logging

Monitoring a live system, with or without machine learning components, means collecting and aggregating data about its states. Nowadays, as production infrastructures are getting more and more complex, with several models deployed simultaneously across several servers, an effective logging system is more important than ever.

Data from these environments needs to be centralized to be analyzed and monitored, either automatically or manually. This will enable continuous improvement of the ML system. An event log of a machine learning system is a record with a timestamp and the following information.

Model metadata
Identification of the model and the version.

Model inputs
Feature values of new observations, which allow for verification of whether the new incoming data is what the model was expecting and thus allowing for detection of data drift (as explained in the previous section).

Model outputs
Predictions made by the model that, along with the ground truth collected later on, give a concrete idea about the model performance in a production environment.

System action
It's rare that the model prediction is the end product of a machine learning application; the more common situation is that the system will take an action based on this prediction. For example, in a fraud detection use case, when the model gives high probability, the system can either block the transaction or send a warning to

the bank. This type of information is important because it affects the user reaction and thus indirectly affects the feedback data.

Model explanation

In some highly regulated domains such as finance or healthcare, predictions must come with an explanation (i.e., which features have the most influence on the prediction). This kind of information is usually computed with techniques such as Shapley value computation and should be logged to identify potential issues with the model (e.g., bias, overfitting).

Model Evaluation

Once the logging system is in place, it periodically fetches data from the production environment for monitoring. Everything goes well until one day the data drift alert is triggered: the incoming data distribution is drifting away from the training data distribution. It's possible that the model performance is degrading.

After review, data scientists decide to improve the model by retraining it, using the techniques described earlier in this chapter. With several trained candidate models, the next step is to compare them with the deployed model. In practice, this means evaluating all the models (the candidates as well as the deployed model) on the same dataset. If one of the candidate models outperforms the deployed model, there are two ways to proceed: either update the model on the production environment or move to an online evaluation via a champion/challenger or A/B testing setup.

In a nutshell, this is the notion of model store. It is a structure that allows data scientists to:

- Compare multiple, newly trained model versions against existing deployed versions
- Compare completely new models against versions of other models on labeled data
- Track model performance over time

Formally, the model evaluation store serves as a structure that centralizes the data related to model life cycle to allow comparisons (though note that comparing models makes sense only if they address the same problem). By definition, all these comparisons are grouped under the umbrella of a logical model.

Logical model

Building a machine learning application is an iterative process, from deploying to production, monitoring performance, retrieving data, and looking for ways to improve how the system addresses the target problem. There are many ways to iterate, some of which have already been discussed in this chapter, including:

- Retraining the same model on new data
- Adding new features to the model
- Developing new algorithms

For those reasons, the machine learning model itself is not a static object; it constantly changes with time. It is therefore helpful to have a higher abstraction level to reason about machine learning applications, which is referred to as a *logical model*.

A logical model is a collection of model templates and their versions that aims to solve a business problem. A model version is obtained by training a model template on a given dataset. All versions of model templates of the same logical model can usually be evaluated on the same kinds of datasets (i.e., on datasets with the same feature definition and/or schema); however, this may not be the case if the problem did not change but the features available to solve it did. Model versions could be implemented using completely different technologies, and there could even be several implementations of the same model version (Python, SQL, Java, etc.); regardless, they are supposed to give the same prediction if given the same input.

Let's get back to the wine example introduced earlier in this chapter. Three months after deployment, there is new data about less alcoholic wine. We can retrain our model on the new data, thus obtaining a new model version using the same model template. While investigating the result, we discover new patterns are emerging. We may decide to create new features that capture this information and add it to the model, or we may decide to use another ML algorithm (like deep learning) instead of XGBoost. This would result in a new model template.

As a result, our model has two model templates and three versions:

- The first version is live in production, based on the original model template.
- The second version is based on the original template, but trained on new data.
- The third version uses the deep learning–based template with additional features and is trained on the same data as the second version.

The information about the evaluation of these versions on various datasets (both the test datasets used at training time and the development datasets that may be scored after training) is then stored in the model evaluation store.

Model evaluation store

As a reminder, model evaluation stores are structures that centralize the data related to model life cycles to allow comparisons. The two main tasks of a model evaluation store are:

- Versioning the evolution of a logical model through time. Each logged version of the logical model must come with all the essential information concerning its training phase, including:

  — The list of features used

  — The preprocessing techniques that are applied to each feature

  — The algorithm used, along with the chosen hyperparameters

  — The training dataset

  — The test dataset used to evaluate the trained model (this is necessary for the version comparison phase)

  — Evaluation metrics

- Comparing the performance between different versions of a logical model. To decide which version of a logical model to deploy, all of them (the candidates and the deployed one) must be evaluated on the same dataset.

The choice of dataset to evaluate is crucial. If there is enough new labeled data to give a reliable estimation of the model performance, this is the preferred choice because it is closest to what we are expecting to receive in the production environment. Otherwise, we can use the original test dataset of the deployed model. Assuming that the data has not drifted, this gives us a concrete idea about the performance of the candidate models compared to the original model.

After identifying the best candidate model, the job is not yet done. In practice, there is often a substantial discrepancy between the offline and online performance of the models. Therefore, it's critical to take the testing to the production environment. This online evaluation gives the most truthful feedback about the behavior of the candidate model when facing real data.

Online Evaluation

Online evaluation of models in production is critical from a business perspective, but can be challenging from a technical perspective. There two main modes of online evaluation:

- Champion/challenger (otherwise known as shadow testing), where the candidate model shadows the deployed model and scores the same live requests
- A/B testing, where the candidate model scores a portion of the live requests and the deployed model scores the others

Both cases require ground truth, so the evaluation will necessarily take longer than the lag between prediction and ground truth obtention. In addition, whenever shadow testing is possible, it should be used over A/B testing because it is far simpler to understand and set up, and it detects differences more quickly.

Champion/Challenger

Champion/challenger involves deploying one or several additional models (the challengers) to the production environment. These models receive and score the same incoming requests as the active model (the champion). However, they do not return any response or prediction to the system: that's still the job of the old model. The predictions are simply logged for further analysis. That's why this method is also called "shadow testing" or "dark launch."

This setup allows for two things:

- Verification that the performance of the new models is better than, or at least as good as, the old model. Because the two models are scoring on the same data, there is a direct comparison of their accuracy in the production environment. Note that this could also be done offline by using the new models on the dataset made of new requests scored by the champion model.

- Measurement of how the new models handle realistic load. Because the new models can have new features, new preprocessing techniques, or even a new algorithm, the prediction time for a request won't be the same as that of the original model, and it is important to have a concrete idea of this change. Of course, this is the main advantage of doing it online.

The other advantage of this deployment scheme is that the data scientist or the ML engineer is giving visibility to other stakeholders on the future champion model: instead of being locked in the data science environment, the challenger model results are exposed to the business leaders, which decreases the perceived risk to switch to a new model.

To be able to compare the champion and the challenger models, the same information must be logged for both, including input data, output data, processing time, etc. This means updating the logging system so that it can differentiate between the two sources of data.

How long should both models be deployed before it's clear that one is better than the other? Long enough that the metric fluctuations due to randomness are dampened because enough predictions have been made. This can be assessed graphically by checking that the metric estimations are not fluctuating anymore or by doing a proper statistical test (as most metrics are averages of row-wise scores, the most usual test is a paired sample T-test) that yields the probability that the observation that one metric is higher than the other is due to these random fluctuations. The wider the metric difference, the fewer predictions necessary to ensure that the difference is significant.

Depending on the use case and the implementation of the champion/challenger system, server performance can be a concern. If two memory-intensive models are called synchronously, they can slow the system down. This will not only have a negative impact on the user experience but also corrupt the data collected about the functioning of the models.

Another concern is communication with the external system. If the two models use an external API to enrich their features, that doubles the number of requests to these services, thus doubling costs. If that API has a caching system in place, then the second request will be processed much faster than the first, which can bias the result when comparing the total prediction time of the two models. Note that the challenger may be used only for a random subset of the incoming requests, which will alleviate the load at the expense of increased time before a conclusion can be drawn.

Finally, when implementing a challenger model, it's important to ensure it doesn't have any influence on the system's actions. This implies two scenarios:

- When the challenger model encounters an unexpected issue and fails, the production environment will not experience any discontinuation or degradation in terms of response time.
- Actions taken by the system depend only on the prediction of the champion model, and they happen only once. For example, in a fraud detection use case, imagine that by mistake the challenger model is plugged directly into the system, charging each transaction twice—a catastrophic scenario.

In general, some effort needs to be spent on the logging, monitoring, and serving system to ensure the production environment functions as usual and is not impacted by any issues coming from the challenger model.

A/B testing

A/B testing (a randomized experiment testing two variants, A and B) is a widely used technique in website optimization. For ML models, it should be used only when champion/challenger is not possible. This might happen when:

- The ground truth cannot be evaluated for both models. For example, for a recommendation engine, the prediction gives a list of items on which a given customer is likely to click if they are presented. Therefore, it is impossible to know if the customer would have clicked if an item was not presented. In this case, some kind of A/B testing will have to be done, in which some customers will be shown the recommendations of model A, and some the recommendations of model B. Similarly, for a fraud detection model, because heavy work is needed to obtain the ground truth, it may not be possible to do so for the positive predictions of two models; it would increase the workload too much, because some frauds are detected by only one model. As a result, randomly applying only the B model to a small fraction of the requests will allow the workload to remain constant.

- The objective to optimize is only indirectly related to the performance of the prediction. Imagine an ad engine based on an ML model that predicts if a user will click on the ad. Now imagine that it is evaluated on the buy rate, i.e., whether the user bought the product or service. Once again, it is not possible to record the reaction of the user for two different models, so in this case, A/B testing is the only way.

Entire books are dedicated to A/B testing, so this section presents only its main idea and a simple walkthrough. Unlike the champion/challenger framework, with A/B testing, the candidate model returns predictions for certain requests, and the original model handles the other requests. Once the test period is over, statistical tests compare the performance of the two models, and teams can make a decision based on the statistical significance of those tests.

In an MLOps context, some considerations need to be made. A walkthrough of these considerations is presented in Table 7-1.

Table 7-1. Considerations for A/B testing in MLOps

Stage	MLOps consideration
Before the A/B test	Define a clear goal: A quantitative business metric that needs to be optimized, such as click-through rate.
	Define a precise population: Carefully choose a segment for the test along with a splitting strategy that assures no bias between groups. (This is the so-called experimental design or randomized control trial that's been popularized by drug studies.) This may be a random split, or it may be more complex. For example, the situation might dictate that all the requests of a particular customer are handled by the same model.
	Define the statistical protocol: The resulting metrics are compared using statistical tests, and the null hypothesis is either rejected or retained. To make the conclusion robust, teams need to define beforehand the sample size for the desired minimum effect size, which is the minimum difference between the two models' performance metrics. Teams must also fix a test duration (or alternatively have a method to handle multiple tests). Note that with similar sample sizes, the power to detect meaningful differences will be lower than with champion/challenger because unpaired sample tests have to be used. (It is usually impossible to match each request scored with model B to a request scored with model A, whereas with champion/challenger, this is trivial.)
During the A/B test	It is important not to stop the experiment before the test duration is over, even if the statistical test starts to return a significant metric difference. This practice (also called p-hacking) produces unreliable and biased results due to cherry-picking the desired outcome.
After the A/B test	Once the test duration is over, check the collected data to make sure the quality is good. From there, run the statistical tests; if the metric difference is statistically significant in favor of the candidate model, the original model can be replaced with the new version.

Closing Thoughts

Ordinary software is built to satisfy specifications. Once an application is deployed, its ability to fulfill its objective does not degrade. ML models, by contrast, have objectives statistically defined by their performance on a given dataset. As a result, their performance changes, usually for the worse, when the statistical properties of the data change.

In addition to ordinary software maintenance needs (bug correction, release upgrades, etc.), this performance drift has to be carefully monitored. We have seen that performance monitoring based on the ground truth is the cornerstone, while drift monitoring can provide early warning signals. Among possible drift mitigation measures, the workhorse is definitely retraining on new data, while model modification remains an option. Once a new model is ready to be deployed, its improved performance can be validated thanks to shadow scoring or, as a second choice, A/B testing. This enables proving that the new model is better in order to improve the performance of the system.

CHAPTER 8

Model Governance

Mark Treveil

We explored the idea of governance as a set of controls placed on a business in Chapter 3. These goals aim to ensure that the business delivers on its responsibilities to all stakeholders, from shareholders and employees to the public and national governments. The responsibilities include financial, legal, and ethical, and are all underpinned by the desire for fairness.

This chapter goes even more in depth on these topics, shifting from why they matter to how organizations can incorporate them as a part of their MLOps strategy.

Who Decides What Governance the Organization Needs?

National regulations are a key part of a society's framework for safeguarding fairness. But these take considerable time to be agreed upon and implemented; they always reflect a slightly historical understanding of fairness and the challenges to it. Just as with ML models, the past cannot always anticipate the evolving problems of the future.

What most businesses want from governance is to safeguard shareholder investment and to help ensure a suitable ROI, both now and in the future. That means the business has to perform effectively, profitability, and sustainably. The shareholders need clear visibility that customers, employees, and regulatory bodies are happy, and they want reassurances that appropriate measures are in place to detect and manage any difficulties that could occur in the future.

None of this is news, of course, nor specific to MLOps. What is different with ML is that it is a new and often opaque technology that carries many risks, but it is rapidly being embedded in decision-making systems that impact every aspect of our lives. ML systems invent their own statistically driven decision-making processes, often extremely difficult to understand, based on large volumes of data that is thought to represent the real world. It's not hard to see what could go wrong!

Perhaps the most surprising influence on the direction of ML governance is public opinion, which evolves much faster than formal regulation. It follows no formal process or etiquette. It doesn't have to be based on fact or reason. Public opinion determines what products people buy, where they invest their money, and what rules and regulations governments make. Public opinion decides what is fair and what is not.

For example, the agricultural biotechnology companies that developed genetically modified crops felt the power of public opinion painfully in the 1990s. While the arguments rage back and forth about whether there was, or was not, a risk to health, public opinion in Europe swung against genetic modification, and these crops were banned in many European countries. The parallels with ML are clear: ML offers benefits to all and yet brings risks that need to be managed if the public is to trust it. Without public trust, the benefits will not fully materialize.

The general public needs to be reassured that ML is fair. What is considered "fair" is not defined in a rule book, and it is not fixed; it will fluctuate based on events, and it will not always be the same across the world. Right now, opinion on ML is in the balance. Most people prefer getting sensibly targeted ads, they like their cars being able to read speed-limit signs, and improving fraud detection ultimately saves them money.

But there have also been well-publicized scandals that have rocked the public's acceptance of this technology. The Facebook-Cambridge Analytica affair, where the companies used the power of ML to manipulate public opinion on social media, shocked the world. This looked like ML with explicitly malicious intent. Equally worrying have been instances of entirely unintentional harm, where ML black box judgments proved to be unacceptably and illegally biased on criteria such as race or gender, for example in criminal assessment systems (*https://oreil.ly/ddM8A*) and in recruitment tools (*https://oreil.ly/VPWi0*).

If businesses and governments want to reap the benefits of ML, they have to safeguard the public trust in it as well as proactively address the risks. For businesses, this means developing strong governance of their MLOps process. They must assess the risks, determine their own set of fairness values, and then implement the necessary process to manage them. Much of this is simply about good housekeeping with an added focus on mitigating the inherent risks of ML, addressing topics such as data provenance, transparency, bias, performance management, and reproducibility.

Matching Governance with Risk Level

Governance is not a free lunch; it takes effort, discipline, and time.

From the business stakeholders' perspective, governance is likely to slow down the delivery of new models, which may cost the business money. For data scientists, it can look like a lot of bureaucracy that erodes their ability to get things done. In contrast, those responsible for managing risk and the DevOps team managing deployment would argue that strict governance across the board should be mandatory.

Those responsible for MLOps must manage the inherent tension between different user profiles, striking a balance between getting the job done efficiently and protecting against all possible threats. This balance can be found by assessing the specific risk of each project and matching the governance process to that risk level. There are several dimensions to consider when assessing risk, including:

- The audience for the model
- The lifetime of the model and its outcomes
- The impact of the outcomes

This assessment should not only determine the governance measures applied, but also drive the complete MLOps development and deployment tool chain.

For example, a self-service analytics (SSA) project (one consumed by a small internal-only audience and often built by business analysts) calls for relatively lightweight governance. Conversely, a model deployed to a public-facing website making decisions that impact people's lives or company finances requires a very thorough process. This process would consider the type of KPIs chosen by the business, the type of model-building algorithm used for the required level of explainability, the coding tools used, the level of documentation and reproducibility, the level of automated testing, the resilience of the hardware platform, and the type of monitoring implemented.

But the business risk is not always so clear cut. An SSA project that makes a decision that has a long-term impact can also be high risk and can justify stronger governance measures. That's why across the board, teams need well thought out, regularly reviewed strategies for MLOps risk assessment (see Figure 8-1 for a breakdown of project criticality and operationalization approaches).

Project criticality	Operationalization	Builder autonomy	Versioning	Resources separation	SLA and support by IT	Integration to ext. systems
Irregular Ad-hoc usage	SSA with run on design node	☆☆☆	—	—	—	—
Scheduled but can be inoperative for a small amount of time	Self-service development and scheduling	☆☆☆	☆☆☆	☆☆	—	—
Scheduled and requires specific monitoring	Light deployment process with rough QA and scheduling	★	★★★	★★★	★	—
Operational projects that cannot suffer outages	Fully controlled deployment CI/CD	—	★★★	★★★	★★★	★★★

Figure 8-1. Choosing the right kind of operationalization model and MLOps features depending on the project's criticality

Current Regulations Driving MLOps Governance

There is little regulation around the world today specifically aimed at ML and AI. Many existing regulations do, however, have a significant impact on ML governance. These take two forms:

- Industry-specific regulation. This is particularly significant in the finance and pharmaceutical sectors.
- Broad-spectrum regulation, particularly addressing data privacy.

A few of the most pertinent regulations are outlined in the following sections. Their relevance to the challenges of MLOps governance is striking, and these regulations give a good indication of what governance measures will be needed broadly across the industry to establish and maintain trust in ML.

Even for those working in industries that don't have specific regulations, the following sections can give a brief idea of what organizations worldwide, regardless of industry, might face in the future in terms of the level of specificity of control with regards to machine learning.

Pharmaceutical Regulation in the US: GxP

GxP (*https://oreil.ly/eg3J2*) is a collection of quality guidelines (such as the Good Clinical Practice, or GCP, guidelines) and regulations established by the U.S. Food and Drug Administration (FDA), which aim to ensure that bio and pharmaceutical products are safe.

GxP's guidelines focus on:

- Traceability, or the ability to re-create the development history of a drug or medical device.
- Accountability, meaning who has contributed what to the development of a drug and when.
- Data Integrity (DI) (*https://oreil.ly/G_wyS*), or the reliability of data used in development and testing. This is based on the ALCOA principle: attributable, legible, contemporaneous, original, and accurate, and considerations include identifying risks and mitigation strategies.

Financial Model Risk Management Regulation

In finance, model risk is the risk of incurring losses when the models used for making decisions about tradable assets prove to be inaccurate. These models, such as the Black–Scholes model, existed long before the arrival of ML.

Model risk management (MRM) regulation has been driven by the experience of the impact of extraordinary events, such as financial crashes, and the resulting harm to the public and the wider economy if severe losses are incurred. Since the financial crisis of 2007–2008, a large amount of additional regulation has been introduced to force good MRM practices (see Figure 8-2).

The UK Prudential Regulation Authority's (PRA) regulation (*https://oreil.ly/tmxVg*), for example, defines four principles for good MRM:

Model definition
Define a model and record such models in inventory.

Risk governance
Establish model risk governance framework, policies, procedures, and controls.

Life cycle management
Create robust model development, implementation, and usage processes.

Effective challenge
Undertake appropriate model validation and independent review.

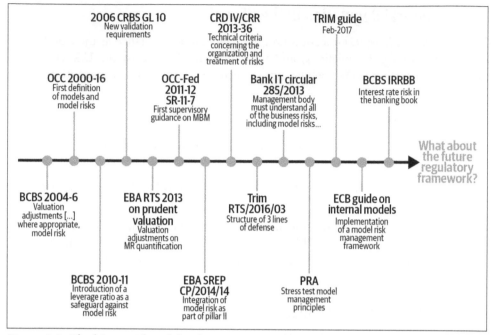

Figure 8-2. *The history of model risk management (MRM) regulation*

GDPR and CCPA Data Privacy Regulations

The EU General Data Protection Regulation (GDPR) was first implemented in 2018, setting guidelines for the collection and processing of personal information from individuals who live in the European Union. However, it was developed with the internet age in mind, so it actually applies for EU visitors to any website, regardless of where that website is based. Since few websites want to exclude EU visitors, sites across the world have been forced to meet the requirements, making GDPR a de facto standard for data protection. The regulations aim to give people control of their personal data that IT systems have collected, including the rights to:

- Be informed about data collected or processed
- Access collected data and understand its processing
- Correct inaccurate data
- Be forgotten (i.e., to have data removed)
- Restrict processing of personal data
- Obtain collected data and reuse it elsewhere
- Object to automated decision-making

The California Consumer Privacy Act (CCPA) is quite similar to GDPR in terms of who and what is protected, although the scope, territorial reach, and financial penalties are all more limited.

The New Wave of AI-Specific Regulations

Around the world, a new wave of regulations and guidelines specifically targeting AI applications (and thus all ML applications) is emerging. The European Union is leading the way with an attempt to establish a framework for trustworthy AI.

In a white paper on artificial intelligence (*https://oreil.ly/rhzo5*), the EU emphasizes the potential benefits of AI for all walks of life. Equally, it highlights that scandals surrounding the misuse of AI and warnings of the dangers of potential advances in the power of AI have not gone unnoticed. The EU considers that regulatory framework based on its fundamental values "will enable it to become a global leader in innovation in the data economy and its applications."

The EU identifies seven key requirements that AI applications should respect to be considered trustworthy:

- Human agency and oversight
- Technical robustness and safety
- Privacy and data governance
- Transparency
- Diversity, non-discrimination, and fairness
- Societal and environmental well-being
- Accountability

The EU approach is not one-size-fits-all: it will primarily impact specific high-risk sectors, including healthcare, transportation, energy, and parts of the public sector. The regulations are expected to be optional for other sectors.

As with GDPR, the EU approach is likely to have a worldwide influence. It is also probable that many large organizations will decide to opt in considering the importance to their businesses of public trust in the use of AI. Even for those not opting in, the framework is likely to establish a way of thinking about governance in AI and will influence their approach.

Table 8-1 outlines some of the statuses of AI governance initiatives across the world. All are following an unmistakably similar route, even if the level of prescriptiveness reflects their traditionally distinct approaches to regulation.

Table 8-1. Status of AI governance initiatives across the world

Regions & organizations	Stage	Focus	Coming next
OECD	Guidance	• 42 signatories • 5 principles for responsible stewardship of trustworthy AI: inclusive growth, human-centered and fairness, transparency and explainability, robustness, and accountability • Recommendations for national policies	
EU	Guidance, communication, direction, and regulation	• Binding for high-risk activities (Sector X impact), optional with possibility for label for others • Specifically targeting model fairness, robustness, and auditability, mixing policies and controls, integrating strong ethical considerations on environmental and social impacts	• Directive by end 2020/early 2021 • To be translated into national regime
Singapore	Guidance	• Positive, nonsanctioned-based approach focusing on practical steps to implementation AI governance at an organization level • Best practice center, supporting AI governance work at Economic Forum level	• Regulation by end 2020/early 2021
US	Guidance, communication, and regulation	• Federal guidelines issued to prepare ground for industry-specific guidelines or regulation • Focus on public trust and fairness; no broader ethics considerations	
UK	Guidance	High-level guidelines only; nonbinding and broad in coverage	
Australia	Guidance	Detailed guidelines issued, integrating ethical and a strong focus on end-consumer protection	

The Emergence of Responsible AI

As the adoption of data science, machine learning, and AI has accelerated worldwide, a loose consensus among AI thinkers has emerged. The most common banner for this consensus is Responsible AI: the idea of developing machine learning systems that are accountable, sustainable, and governable. In essence, AI systems should do what they are supposed to, remain reliable over time, and be well controlled as well as auditable.

There is no strict definition of Responsible AI or the terms used to frame it, but there is agreement about the overarching considerations and largely about what is needed to deliver it (see Table 8-2). Despite the lack of any single body driving the movement, Responsible AI has already had a significant influence on collective thinking, and especially on the EU's trustworthy AI regulators.

Table 8-2. Components of Responsible AI, an increasingly critical part of MLOps

Intentionality	Accountability
Must have:	Must have:
• Assurance that models are designed and behave in ways aligned with their purpose • Assurance that data used for AI projects comes from compliant and unbiased sources plus a collaborative approach to AI projects that ensures multiple checks and balances on potential model bias • Intentionality also includes explainability, meaning the result of AI systems should be explainable by humans (ideally not just the humans that created the system)	• Central control, management, and the ability to audit the enterprise AI effort (no shadow IT!) • An overall view of which teams are using what data, how, and in which models • Trust that data is reliable and being collected in accordance with regulation as well as a centralized understanding of which models are being used for which business process. This is closely tied to traceability—if something goes wrong, is it easy to find where in the pipeline it happened?
Human-centered approach	
Providing people with the tools and training to be aware of and then execute on both components	

Key Elements of Responsible AI

Responsible AI is about the responsibility of data practitioners, not about AI itself being responsible: this is a very important distinction. Another important distinction is that, according to Kurt Muemel of Dataiku, "It is not necessarily about intentional harm, but accidental harm."

This section presents five key elements that figure in Responsible AI thinking—data, bias, inclusiveness, model management at scale, and governance—as well as MLOps considerations for each element.

Element 1: Data

The dependence on data is a fundamental differentiator between ML and traditional software development. The quality of the data used will make the biggest impact on the accuracy of the model. Some real-world considerations are as follows:

- Provenance is king. Understand how the data was collected and its journey to the point of use.
- Get the data off of desktops. Data must be manageable, securable, and traceable. Personal data must be strictly managed.
- The quality of data over time: consistency, completeness, and ownership.
- Bias in, bias out. Biased input data can occur easily and unintentionally.

Element 2: Bias

ML predictive modeling is about building a system to recognize and exploit tendencies in the real world. Certain types of cars, driven by certain types of people, in certain places are more likely to be costlier to insurance companies than others. But is matching a pattern always considered ethical? When is such pattern-matching proportionate, and when is it an unfair bias?

Establishing what is fair is not clear-cut. Even using a churn model to give rebates to the customers who are more likely to leave might be considered as unfair against dormant customers who will pay more for the same product. Regulations are a place to start looking, but as already discussed, opinion is not universal and is not fixed. Even with a clear understanding of the fairness constraints to work toward, achieving them is not simple. When the developers of the recruitment system that was biased against women's schools adapted the model to ignore the words like "women's," they found that even the tone of the language in a resume reflected the gender of the author and created unwanted bias against women (*https://oreil.ly/JEIL7*). Addressing these biases has deep implications on the ML model to be built (see "Impact of Responsible AI on Modeling" on page 53 for a detailed example).

Taking a step back, these bias problems are not new; for example, hiring discrimination has always been an issue. What is new is that, thanks to the IT revolution, data to assess biases is more available. On top of that, thanks to the automation of decision making with machine learning, it is possible to change the behavior without having to go through the filter of individuals making subjective decisions.

The bottom line is that biases are not only statistical. Bias checks should be integrated in governance frameworks so that issues are identified as early as possible, since they do have the potential to derail data science and machine learning projects.

It's not all bad news: there are many potential sources of statistical bias (i.e., of the world as it was) that *can* be addressed by data scientists:

- Is bias encoded into the training data? Is the raw material biased? Has data preparation, sampling, or splitting introduced bias?
- Is the problem framed properly?
- Do we have the right target for all subpopulations? Beware that many variables may be highly correlated.
- Is feedback-loop data biased through factors such as the order in which choices are presented in the UI?

It is so complex to prevent the problems caused by bias that much of the current focus is on detecting bias before it causes harm. ML interpretability is the current mainstay of bias detection, bringing understanding to ML models through a set of technical tools to analyze models including:

- Prediction understanding: Why did a model make a specific prediction?
- Subpopulation analysis: Is there bias among subpopulations?
- Dependency understanding: What contributions are individual features making?

A very different, but complementary, approach to addressing bias is to leverage as broad a range of human expertise as possible in the development process. This is one aspect of the idea of inclusiveness in Responsible AI.

Element 3: Inclusiveness

The human-in-the-loop (HITL) approach aims to combine the best of human intelligence with the best of machine intelligence. Machines are great at making smart decisions from vast datasets, whereas people are much better at making decisions with less information. Human judgment is particularly effective for making ethical and harm-related judgments.

This concept can be applied to the way models are used in production, but it can be equally important in the way models are built. Formalizing human responsibility in the MLOps loop, for example through sign-off processes, can be simple to do, but highly effective.

The principle of inclusiveness takes the idea of human-AI collaboration further: bringing as diverse a set of human expertise to the ML life cycle as possible reduces the risk of serious blind spots and omissions. The less inclusive the group building the ML, the greater the risk.

The perspectives of the business analyst, the subject matter expert, the data scientist, the data engineer, the risk manager, and the technical architect are all different. All of these perspectives together bring far greater clarity to managing model development and deployment than relying on any single user profile, and enabling these user profiles to collaborate effectively is a key factor in reducing risk and increasing the performance of MLOps in any organization. Refer to Chapter 2 for clear examples of collaboration among different profiles for better MLOps performance.

Full inclusiveness may even bring the consumer into the process, perhaps through focus group testing. The objective of inclusiveness is to bring the appropriate human expertise into the process, regardless of source. Leaving ML to data scientists is not the answer to managing risk.

Element 4: Model Management at Scale

Managing the risk associated with ML when there are a handful of models in production can afford to be largely manual. But as the volume of deployments grows, the challenges multiply rapidly. Here are some key considerations for managing ML at scale:

- A scalable model life cycle needs to be largely automated as well as streamlined.
- Errors, for example in a subset of a dataset, will propagate out rapidly and widely.
- Existing software engineering techniques can assist ML at scale.
- Decisions must be explainable, auditable, and traceable.
- Reproducibility is key to understanding what went wrong, who or what was responsible, and who should ensure it is corrected.
- Model performance will degrade over time: monitoring, drift management, retraining, and remodeling must be built into the process.
- Technology is evolving rapidly; an approach to integrating new technologies is required.

Element 5: Governance

Responsible AI sees strong governance as the key to achieving fairness and trustworthiness. The approach builds on traditional governance techniques:

- Determine intentions at the beginning of the process
- Formalize bringing humans in the loop
- Clearly identify responsibilities (Figure 8-3)
- Integrate goals that define and structure the process
- Establish and communicate a process and rules
- Define measurable metrics and monitor for deviation
- Build multiple checks into the MLOps pipeline aligned with overall goals
- Empower people through education
- Teach builders as well as decision makers how to prevent harm

Governance is, therefore, both the foundation and the glue of MLOps initiatives. However, it's important to recognize that it goes beyond the borders of traditional data governance.

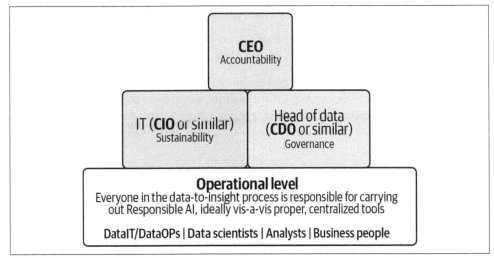

Figure 8-3. A representation of who is responsible at different levels of the organization for different parts of the Responsible AI process

A Template for MLOps Governance

Having explored the key themes to be addressed by an MLOps governance, both through regulatory measures and the Responsible AI movement, it is time to map out how to implement a robust governance framework of MLOps.

There is no one-size-fits-all solution across businesses, and different use cases within a business justify different levels of management, but the step-by-step approach outlined can be applied in any organization to guide the implementation process.

The process has eight steps:

1. Understand and classify the analytics use cases.
2. Establish an ethical position.
3. Establish responsibilities.
4. Determine governance policies.
5. Integrate policies into the MLOps process.
6. Select the tools for centralized governance management.
7. Engage and educate.
8. Monitor and refine.

This section will go through each of the steps in detail, including a simple definition and the "how" of actually implementing the step.

Step 1: Understand and Classify the Analytics Use Cases

This step entails defining what the different classes of analytics use cases are and, subsequently, what the governance needs are for each.

Consider the answers to the following questions for a representative cross-section of analytics use cases. Identify the key distinguishing features of the different use cases and categorize these features. Conflate categories where appropriate. Typically, it will be necessary to associate several categories to each use case to fully describe it.

- What regulations is each use case subject to, and what are the implications? Sector-specific regulations, regional, PII?
- Who consumes the results of the model? The public? One of many internal users?
- What are the availability requirements for the deployed model? 24/7 real-time scoring, scheduled batch scoring, ad-hoc runs (self-service analytics)?
- What is the impact of any errors and deficiencies? Legal, financial, personal, public trust?
- What is the cadence and urgency of releases?
- What is the lifetime of the model and the lifetime of the impact of its decision?
- What is the likely rate of model quality decay?
- What is the need for explainability and transparency?

Step 2: Establish an Ethical Position

We established that fairness and ethical considerations are important motivating factors for effective governance, that businesses have a choice on their ethical stance, and that this impacts public perception and trust. The position a business takes is a trade-off between the cost to implement the position and public perception. Responsible stances rarely come at zero short-term financial cost even if the long-term ROI may be positive.

Any MLOps governance framework needs to reflect the ethical position of the company. While the position typically impacts what a model does and how it does it, the MLOps governance process needs to ensure that deployed models match the chosen ethical stance. This stance is likely to influence the governance process more widely, including the selection and verification of new models and the acceptable likelihood of accidental harm.

Consider the following ethical questions:

- What aspects of well-being in society matter? E.g., equality, privacy, human rights and dignity, employment, democracy, bias
- Is the potential impact on human psychology to be considered? E.g., human-human or human-AI relationships, deception, manipulation, exploitation
- Is a stance on the financial impact required? E.g., market manipulation
- How transparent should the decision making be?
- What level of accountability for AI-driven mistakes does the business want to accept?

Step 3: Establish Responsibilities

Identify the groups of people responsible for overseeing MLOps governance as well as their roles.

- Engage the whole organization, across departments, from top to bottom of the management hierarchy.
- Peter Drucker's famous line "Culture eats strategy for breakfast" highlights the power of broad engagement and shared beliefs.
- Avoid creating all-new governance structures. Look at what structures exist already and try to incorporate MLOps governance into them.
- Get senior management sponsorship for the governance process.
- Think in terms of separate levels of responsibility:
  — Strategic: set out the vision
  — Tactical: implement and enforce the vision
  — Operational: execute on a daily basis
- Consider building a RACI matrix for the complete MLOps process (see Figure 8-4). RACI stands for *responsible, accountable, consulted, informed,* and it highlights the roles of different stakeholders in the overall MLOps process. It is quite likely that any matrix you create at this stage will need to be refined later on in the process.

Tasks	Business stakeholders	Business analysis/citizen DS	Data scientists	Risk/audit	Data ops	Production/exploitation	Resources admin/architect
Identification	A/R	C		I			
Data preparation	C	A/R	C				
Data modeling	C	A	R				
Model acceptance	I	C	C	A/R			
Productionalization		C	A/R	I	C		
Capitalization			R		R		A
Integration to external systems					A/R		
Global orchestration		C			R	A	
User acceptance tests	A/R	R	C		I		
Deployments					R	A	I
Monitoring	I	C				A/R	I

A: accountable   R: responsible   C: consulted   I: informed

Figure 8-4. A typical RACI matrix for MLOps

Step 4: Determine Governance Policies

With an understanding of the scope and objectives for governance now established, and the engagement of the responsible governance leaders, it is time to consider the core policies for the MLOps process. This is no small task, and it is unlikely to be achieved in one iteration. Focus on establishing the broad areas of policy and accept that experience will help to evolve the details.

Consider the classification of initiatives from Step 1. What governance measures do the team or organization need in each case?

In initiatives where there is less concern about the risk or regulatory compliance, lighter-weight, cheaper measures may be appropriate. For example, "what if" calculations to determine the number of in-flight meals of different types has relatively little impact—after all, the mix was never right even before the introduction of machine learning. Even such a seemingly insignificant use case may have ethical implications as meal choices are likely to be correlated to religion or gender, which are protected attributes in many countries. On the other hand, the implications of calculations to determine the level of fueling of planes carry substantially greater risk.

Governance considerations can be broadly grouped under the headings in Table 8-3. For each heading, there are a range of measures to consider for each class.

Table 8-3. MLOps governance considerations

Governance consideration	Example measures
Reproducibility and traceability	Full VM and data snapshot for precise and rapid model re-instantiation, *or* ability to re-create the environment and retrain with a data sample, *or* only record metrics of models deployed?
Audit and documentation	Full log of all changes during development including experiments run and reasons for choices made *or* automated documentation of deployed model only *or* no documentation at all
Human-in-the-loop sign-off	Multiple sign-offs for every environment move (development, QA, preproduction, production)
Preproduction verification	Verify model documentation by hand-coding the model and comparing results *or* full automated test pipeline re-creating in production-like environment with extensive unit and end-to-end test cases *or* automated checks on database, software version, and naming standards only
Transparency and explainability	Use manually-coded decision tree for maximum explainability *or* use regression algorithms' explainability tools such as Shapely values *or* accept opaque algorithms such as neural networks
Bias and harm testing	"Red team" adversarial manual testing using multiple tools and attack vectors *or* automated bias checking on specific subpopulations
Production deployment modes	Containerized deployment to elastic scalable high-availability, multi-node configuration with automated stress/load testing prior to deployment *or* a single production server
Production monitoring	Real-time alerting of errors, dynamic multi-armed bandit model balancing, automated nightly retraining, model evaluation, and redeployment *or* weekly input drift monitoring and manual retraining *or* basic infrastructure alerts, no monitoring, no feedback-based retraining
Data quality and compliance	PII considerations including anonymization *and* documented and reviewed column-level lineage to understand the source, quality, and appropriateness of the data *and* automated data quality checks for anomalies

The finalized governance policies should provide:

- A process for determining the classification of any analytics initiative. This could be implemented as a checklist or a risk assessment application.
- A matrix of initiative classification against governance consideration, where each cell identifies the measures required.

Step 5: Integrate Policies into the MLOps Process

Once the governance policies for the different classes of initiatives have been identified, measures to implement them need to be incorporated into the MLOps process and responsibilities for actioning the measures assigned.

While most businesses will have an existing MLOps process, it is quite likely that this has not been defined explicitly, but rather has evolved in response to individual needs. Now is the time to revisit, enhance, and document the process. Successful adoption of the governance process can only happen if it is communicated clearly and buy-in is sought from each stakeholder group.

Understand all of the steps in the existing process by interviewing those responsible. Where there is no existing formal process, this is often harder than it sounds because the process steps are often not explicitly defined, and ownership is unclear.

Attempting to map the policy-driven governance measures into the understanding of the process will identify issues in the process very quickly. Within one business there may be a range of different styles of project and governance needs, such as:

- One-off self-service analytics
- Internally consumed models
- Models embedded in public websites
- Models deployed to Internet of Things devices

In these cases, the differences between some processes may be so great it is best to think in terms of several parallel processes. Ultimately, every governance measure for each use case should be associated with a process step and with a team that is ultimately responsible, as presented here:

Process step	Example activities and governance considerations
Business scoping	Record objectives, define KPIs, and record sign-off: for internal governance considerations
Ideation	Data discovery: data quality and regulatory compliance constraints Algorithm choice: impacted by explainability requirements
Development	Data preparation: consider PII compliance, separation of legal regional scopes, avoid input bias Model development: consider model reproducibility and auditabilityModel testing and verification: bias and harm testing, explainability
Preproduction	Verify performance/bias with production data Production-ready testing: verify scalability
Deployment	Deployment strategy: driven by the level of operationalization Deployment verification testsUse of shadow challenger or A/B test techniques for in-production verification
Monitoring and feedback	Performance metrics and alerting Prediction log analysis for input drift with alerting

Step 6: Select the Tools for Centralized Governance Management

The MLOps governance process impacts both the complete ML life cycle and many teams across the organization. Each step requires a specific sequence of actions and checks to be executed. Traceability of both the development of the model and the execution of governance activities is a complex challenge.

Most organizations still have a "paper form" mindset for process management, where forms are filled in, circulated, signed, and filed. The forms may be text documents, circulated via email, and filed electronically, but the limitations of paper remain. It is hard to track progress, associate artifacts, review many projects at once, prompt for action, and remind teams of responsibilities. The complete record of events is typically spread across multiple systems and owned by individual teams, making a simple overview of analytics projects effectively impossible.

While teams will always have tools specific to their roles, MLOps governance is much more effective if the overarching process is managed and tracked from one system. This system should:

- Centralize the definition of the governance process flows for each class of analytics use cases
- Enable tracking and enforcement of the complete governance process
- Provide a single point of reference for the discovery of analytics projects
- Enable collaboration between teams, in particular, the transfer of work between teams
- Integrate with existing tools used for project execution

The current workflow, project management, and MLOps tools can only partially support these objectives. A new category of ML governance tools is emerging to support this need directly and more fully. These new tools focus on the specific challenges of ML governance, including:

- A single view of the status of all models (otherwise known as a model registry)
- Process gates with a sign-off mechanism to allow ready traceability of the history of decision making
- Ability to track all versions of a model
- Ability to link to artifact stores, metrics snapshots, and documentation
- Ability to tailor processes specifically for each class of analytics use cases
- Ability to integrate health monitoring from production systems and to track the performance of models against the original business KPIs

Step 7: Engage and Educate

Without a program of engagement and training for the groups involved in overseeing and executing the governance process, the chances of it being even partially adopted are slim. It is essential that the importance of MLOps governance to the business, and the necessity of each team's contribution, is communicated. Building on this understanding, every individual needs to learn what they must do, when, and how.

This exercise will require considerable documentation, training, and, most of all, time.

Start by communicating the broad vision for MLOps governance in the business. Highlight the dangers of the status quo, outline a process, and detail how it is tailored to the range of use cases.

Engage directly with each team involved and build a training program directly with them. Do not be afraid to leverage their experience to shape not only the training, but also the detailed implementation of their governance responsibilities. The result will be much stronger buy-in and more effective governance.

Step 8: Monitor and Refine

Is the newly implemented governance working? Are the prescribed steps being implemented, and are the objectives being met? What actions should be taken if things are going poorly? How do we measure the gap between today's reality and where the business needs to be?

Measuring success requires metrics and checks. It requires people to be tasked with monitoring and a way to address problems. The governance process and the way it is implemented will need to be refined over time, based both on lessons learned and on evolving requirements (including, as discussed earlier in this chapter, evolving regulatory requirements).

A big factor in the success of the process will be the diligence of the individuals responsible for the individual measures in the process, and incentivizing them is key.

Monitoring the governance process starts with a clear understanding of the key performance metrics and targets—KPIs for governance. These should aim to measure both whether the process is being enacted and whether objectives are being achieved. Monitoring and auditing can be time consuming, so look to automate metrics as far as possible and encourage individual teams to own the monitoring of metrics that relate to their area of responsibility.

It's hard to make people carry out tasks that seemingly deliver nothing concrete to those doing the work. One popular tactic to address this is gamification. This is not about making everything look like a video game, but about introducing incentives for people to carry out tasks where the main benefit is derived by others.

Look to gamify the governance process in simple ways: publishing KPI results widely is the simplest place to start. Just being able to see targets being met is a source of satisfaction and motivation. Leaderboards, whether at the team or individual level, can add some constructive element of competition. For example, people whose work consistently passes compliance checks the first time, or meets deadlines, should be able to feel their efforts are visible.

However, excessive competition can be disruptive and demotivating. A balance must be struck, and this is best achieved by building up gamification elements slowly over time. Start with the least competition-oriented and add new elements one by one, measuring their effectiveness before adding the next.

Monitoring changes in the governance landscape is essential. This might be regulatory, or it might be about public opinion. Those with responsibility for the strategic vision must continue to monitor it as well as have a process to evaluate potential changes.

Finally, all monitoring of the process is only worthwhile if issues are acted upon. Establish a process for agreeing on change and for enacting it. This may result in revisiting policies, processes, tools, responsibilities, education, and monitoring! It's necessary to iterate and refine, but the balance between efficiency and effectiveness is hard to find; many lessons can only be learned the hard way. Build a culture where people see iteration and refinement as a measure of a successful process, not a failed one.

Closing Thoughts

It's hard to separate MLOps from its governance. It's not possible to successfully manage the model life cycle, mitigate the risks, and deliver value at scale without governance. Governance impacts everything from how the business can acceptably exploit ML, to the data and algorithms that can be used, to the style of operationalization, monitoring, and retraining.

MLOps at scale is in its infancy. Few businesses are doing it, and even fewer are doing it well. While governance is the key to improving the effectiveness of MLOps, there are few tools today that directly address this challenge, and there is only piecemeal advice.

Public trust in ML is at risk. Even slow-moving organizations like the EU understand this. If trust is lost, then so too will be many of the benefits to be derived from ML. Additional legislation is being prepared, but even without this, businesses need to worry about the potential damage to their public image that can be caused by an inadvertently harmful model.

When planning to scale MLOps, start with governance and use it to drive the process. Don't bolt it on at the end. Think through the policies; think about using tooling to give a centralized view; engage across the organization. It will take time and iteration, but ultimately the business will be able to look back and be proud that it took its responsibilities seriously.

MLOps: Real-World Examples

CHAPTER 9

MLOps in Practice: Consumer Credit Risk Management

In the final chapters of this book, we explore three examples of how MLOps might look in practice. We explicitly chose these three examples because they represent fundamentally different use cases for machine learning and illustrate how MLOps methodology might differ to suit the needs of the business and its ML model life cycle practices.

Background: The Business Use Case

When a consumer asks for a loan, the credit institution has to make a decision on whether or not to grant it. Depending on the case, the amount of automation in the process may vary. However, it is very likely that the decision will be informed by scores that estimate the probability that the loan will or will not be repaid as expected.

Scores are routinely used at different stages of the process:

- At the prescreen stage, a score computed with a small number of features allows the institution to quickly discard some applications.
- At the underwriting stage, a score computed with all the required information gives a more precise basis for the decision.
- After the underwriting stage, scores can be used to assess the risk associated with loans in the portfolio.

Analytics methods have been used for decades to compute these probabilities. For example, the FICO score has been used since 1995 in the United States. Given the direct impact they have on the institutions' revenues and on customers' lives, these predictive models have always been under great scrutiny. Consequently, processes, methods, and skills have been formalized into a highly regulated environment to ensure the sustainable performance of models.

Whether the models are based on expert-made rules, on classical statistical models, or on more recent machine learning algorithms, they all have to comply with similar regulations. Consumer credit risk management can therefore be seen as a precursor of MLOps: parallels with other use cases as well as best practices can be analyzed based on this use case.

At the time a credit decision is made, information about the customer's historical and current situation is usually available. How much credit does the customer hold? Has the customer ever not repaid a loan (in credit jargon, is the customer a delinquent)? In some countries, organizations called credit bureaus collect this information and make it available to creditors either directly or through the form of a score (like the aforementioned FICO score).

The definition of the target to be predicted is more complex. A customer not repaying as expected is a "bad" outcome in credit risk modeling. In theory, one should wait for the complete repayment to determine a "good" outcome and for the loss charge off to determine a "bad" outcome. However, it may take a long time to obtain these ultimate figures, and waiting for them would deter reactivity to changing conditions. As a result, trade-offs are usually made, based on various indicators, to declare "bad" outcomes before the losses are certain.

Model Development

Historically, credit risk modeling is based on a mix of rules ("manual feature engineering" in modern ML jargon) and logistic regression. Expert knowledge is vital to creating a good model. Building adapted customer segmentation as well as studying the influence of each variable and the interactions between variables requires enormous time and effort. Combined with advanced techniques like two-stage models with offset, advanced general linear models based on Tweedie distribution, or monotonicity constraints on one side and financial risk management techniques on the other side, this makes the field a playground for actuaries.

Gradient boosting algorithms like XGBoost have reduced the cost to build good models. However, their validation is made more complex by the black box effect: it's hard to get the feeling that such models give sensible results whatever the inputs. Nevertheless, credit risk modelers have learned to use and validate these new types of models. They have developed new validation methodologies based, for example, on individual explanations (e.g., Shapley values) to build trust into their models, which is a critical component of MLOps, as we've explored throughout this book.

Model Bias Considerations

The modeler also has to take into account selection biases, as the model will inevitably be used to reject applicants. As a result, the population to which a loan is granted is not representative of the applicant population.

By training a model version on the population selected by the previous model version without care, the data scientist would make a model unable to accurately predict on the rejected population because it is not represented in the training dataset, while it is exactly what is expected from the model. This effect is called cherry-picking. As a result, special methods, like reweighting based on the applicant population or calibrating the model based on external data, have to be used.

Models that are used for risk assessment and not only to make decisions about granting loans have to produce probabilities and not only yes/no outcomes. Usually, the probability produced directly by prediction models is not accurate. While it is not an issue if data scientists apply thresholding to obtain a binary classification, they will usually need a monotonous transformation called a *calibration* to recover "true" probabilities as evaluated on historical data.

The model validation for this use case typically consists of:

- Testing its performance on out-of-sample datasets, chosen after (or, in some cases, before, as well) the training datasets.
- Investigating the performance not only overall, but also per subpopulation. The subpopulations would typically have customer segments based on revenue, and with the rise of Responsible AI, other segmenting variables like gender or any protected attribute according to local regulation. Risks of not doing so can result in serious damages, as Apple learned the hard way in 2019 when its credit card was said to be "sexist" against women applying for credit (*https://oreil.ly/iO3yj*).

Prepare for Production

Given the significant impact of credit risk models, their validation process involves significant work with regard to the modeling part of the life cycle, and it includes the full documentation of:

- The data used
- The model and the hypothesis made to build it
- The validation methodology and the validation results
- The monitoring methodology

The monitoring methodology in this scenario is twofold: data and performance drift. As the delay between the prediction and obtaining the ground truth is long (typically the duration of the loan plus a few months to take into account late payments), it is not enough to monitor the model performance: data drift also has to be monitored carefully.

For example, should an economic recession occur or should the commercial policy change, it is likely that the applicant population would change in such a way that the model's performance could not be guaranteed without further validation. Data drift is usually performed by customer segment with generic statistical metrics that measure distances between probability distributions (like Kolmogorov-Smirnov or Wasserstein distances) and also with metrics that are specific to financial services, like population stability index and characteristic stability index. Performance drift is also regularly assessed on subpopulations (*https://oreil.ly/1-7kd*) with generic metrics (AUC) or specific metrics (Kolmogorov-Smirnov, Gini).

The model documentation is usually reviewed by an MRM team in a very formal and standalone process. Such an independent review is a good practice to make sure that the right questions are asked of the model development team. In some critical cases, the validation team may rebuild the model from scratch given the documentation. In some cases, the second implementation is made using an alternative technology to establish confidence in documented understanding of the model and to highlight unseen bugs deriving from the original toolset.

Complex and time-consuming model validation processes have an implication on the entire MLOps life cycle. Quick-fixes and rapid model iteration are not possible with such lengthy QA and lead to a very slow and deliberate MLOps life cycle.

Deploy to Production

In a typical large financial services organization, the production environment is not only separate from the design environment, but also likely to be based on a different technical stack. The technical stack for critical operations—like transaction validation, but also potentially loan validation—will always evolve slowly.

Historically, the production environments have mainly supported rules and linear models like logistic regression. Some can handle more complex models such as PMML or JAR file. For less critical use cases, Docker deployment or deployment through integrated data science and machine learning platforms may be possible. As a result, the operationalization of the model may involve operations that range from clicking on a button to writing a formula based on a Microsoft Word document.

Activity logging of the deployed model is essential for monitoring model performance in such a high-value use case. Depending on the frequency of the monitoring, the feedback loop may be automated or not. For example, automation may not be necessary if the task is performed only once or twice a year and the largest amount of time is spent asking questions of the data. On the other hand, automation might be essential if the assessment is done weekly, which may be the case for short-term loans with durations of a few months.

Closing Thoughts

Financial services have been developing schemes for prediction model validation and monitoring for decades. They have been able to continuously adapt to new modeling technologies like gradient boosting methods. Given their important impact, the processes around the life cycle management of these models are well formalized and even incorporated into many regulations. As a result, they can be a source of best practices for MLOps in other domains, though adaptations are needed as the trade-off between robustness on one side and cost efficiency, time to value, and—importantly—team frustration on the other may be different in other businesses.

CHAPTER 10

MLOps in Practice: Marketing Recommendation Engines

Makoto Miyazaki

Recommendation engines have become very popular in the last 20 years, from the first Amazon book recommendations to today's generalized use in digital shops, advertisements, and music and video streaming. We have all become accustomed to them. However, throughout the years, the underlying technologies behind these recommendation engines have evolved.

This chapter covers a use case that illustrates the adaption of and need for MLOps strategies given the particularities of a fast-paced and rapidly changing machine learning model life cycle.

The Rise of Recommendation Engines

Historically, marketing recommendations were human-built. Based on qualitative and quantitative marketing studies, marketing moguls would set up rules that statically defined the impression (in the sense of advertising views) sent to a customer with given characteristics. This technique gave rise to the marketing data mining urban legend (*https://oreil.ly/HDPpE*) that a grocery chain discovered that men who bought diapers on Thursdays and Saturdays were more likely to buy beer as well and hence placing the two next to each other will increase beer sales.

Overall, recommendation engines created manually presented numerous bottlenecks that resulted in a significant amount of wasted money: it was hard to build rules based on many different customer features because the rule creation process was manual, it was hard to set up experiments to test many different kinds of impressions, and it was hard to update the rules when the behavior of the customers changed.

The Role of Machine Learning

The rise of ML has brought a new paradigm to recommendation engines, allowing for the elimination of rules based on human insight. A new class of algorithm called *collaborative filtering* dominates the field. This algorithm is able to analyze customer and purchase data with millions of customers and tens of thousands of products to perform recommendations without any prior marketing knowledge. By identifying efficiently what customers that look like the current customer bought, marketers can rely on automatic strategies that outperform traditional ones both in cost and efficiency.

Because the process of building strategies is automatic, it is possible to update them regularly and to compare them using A/B testing or shadow scoring schemes (including the way to choose the impression among all possibilities). Note that these algorithms may be combined with more classical business rules for various reasons—e.g., avoiding the filtering bubble, not selling a product in a given geographical area, or preventing the use of a specific association that is statistically meaningful but unethical to use (like proposing alcohol to a recovering alcoholic), to name a few.

Push or Pull?

When implementing a recommendation engine, it is important to keep in mind that its structure will depend on whether the recommendations are pushed or pulled. Push channels are the easiest to handle; for example, they can consist of sending emails or making outbound calls.

The recommendation engine can be run on a regular basis in batch mode (typically between once a day and once a month), and it is easy to split the customer dataset into several parts to perform analysis within a sound experimental design. The regularity of the process allows for regular review and optimization of the strategy.

Pull channels are often more effective because they provide information to customers when they need it—for example, when doing an online search or when calling a customer service line. Specific information from the session can be used (e.g., what the user has searched for) to precisely tailor the recommendation. Music streaming platforms, for instance, provide pull-channel recommendations for playlists.

Recommendations can be prebaked, as illustrated in the in-depth example in this chapter, or made in real time. In the latter case, a special architecture has to be set up to compute recommendations on the fly.

Comparing strategies in a pull context is more challenging. First, the customers who call in on a given channel are likely to differ from the average customer. In simple cases, it is possible to randomly choose the strategy to use for each recommendation, but it also happens that the strategy needs to be used consistently over a given period for a given customer. This usually results in an unbalanced proportion of recommendations made with each strategy, which makes the statistical treatment to decide which one is the best more complex. However, once a good framework is set, this allows a very quick improvement cycle, as many strategies can be tested in real time.

Data Preparation

The customer data that is usually accessible to a recommendation engine is composed of the following:

- Structural information about the customer (e.g., age, gender, location)
- Information about historical activities (e.g., past views, purchases, searches)
- Current context (e.g., current search, viewed product)

Whatever the technique used, all customer information has to be aggregated into a vector (a list of fixed size) of characteristics. For example, from the historical activities, the following characteristics could be extracted:

- Amount of purchases during the last week or the last month
- Number of views during past periods
- Increase in spending or in views during the last month
- Previously seen impressions and customer's response

In addition to customer data, the recommendation context can also be taken into account. For example, days to summer for seasonal products like above-ground swimming pools or days to monthly pay day, as some customers delay purchases for cash flow reasons.

Once the customer and context data is formatted, it is important to define the set of possible recommendations, and there are many choices to make. The same product may be presented with different offers, which may be communicated in different ways.

It is of the utmost importance not to forget the "do not recommend anything" option. Indeed, most of us have the personal experience that not all recommendations have a positive impact. Sometimes not showing anything might be better than the alternatives. It's also important to consider that some customers may not be entitled to see certain recommendations, for example depending on their geographical origin.

Design and Manage Experiments

To leverage the continuous improvement potential of recommendation engines, it is necessary to experiment with different strategies within a sound framework. When designing a prediction model for a recommendation engine, the data scientist might well focus on a simple strategy, such as predicting the probability that a given customer clicks on a given recommendation.

This may seem a reasonable compromise compared to the more precise approach of trying to gather information about whether the customer purchased the product and whether to attribute this purchase to a given recommendation. However, this is not adequate from a business perspective, as phenomena like cannibalization may occur (i.e., by showing a low-margin product to a customer, one might prevent them from buying a high-margin product). As a result, even if the predictions were good and resulted in increased sales volume, the overall revenue might be reduced.

On the other hand, bluntly promoting the organization's interest and not the customer's could also have detrimental long-term consequences. The overarching KPI that is used to assess if a given strategy yields better results should be carefully chosen, together with the time period over which it is evaluated. Choosing the revenue over a two-week period after the recommendation as the main KPI is common practice.

To be as close as possible to an experimental setting, also called A/B testing, the control group and the experimental groups have to be carefully chosen. Ideally, the groups are defined before the start of the experiment by randomly splitting the customer base. If possible, customers should not have been involved in another experimentation recently so that their historical data is not polluted by its impact. However, this may not be possible in a pull setting in which many new customers are coming in. In this case, the assignment could be decided on the fly. The size of the groups as well as the duration of the experiments depend on the expected magnitude of the KPI difference between the two groups: the larger the expected effect, the smaller the group size and the shorter the duration.

The experimentation could also be done in two steps: in the first one, two groups of equal but limited size could be selected. If the experimentation is positive, the deployment could start with 10% on the new strategy, a proportion that can be raised progressively if results are in line with expectations.

Model Training and Deployment

To better illustrate the MLOps process for this type of use case, the following sections focus on the specific example of a hypothetical company deploying an automated pipeline to train and deploy recommendation engines. The company is a global software company (let's call it MarketCloud) headquartered in Silicon Valley.

One of MarketCloud's products is a software-as-a-service (SaaS) platform called SalesCore. SalesCore is a B2B product that allows its users (businesses) to drive sales to customers in a simple manner by keeping track of deals, clearing tedious administration tasks off their desks, and creating customized product offers for each customer (see Figure 10-1).

From time to time, MarketCloud's clients use the cloud-based SalesCore while on a call with their customers, adjusting their sales strategy by looking at past interactions with the customers as well as at the product offers and discounts suggested by SalesCore.

MarketCloud is a mid-sized company with an annual revenue of around $200 million and a few thousand employees. From salespeople at a brewing company to those in a telecommunication entity, MarketCloud's clients represent a range of businesses.

Figure 10-1. Mock-up of the SalesCore platform, the basis of the theoretical company on which this section's example is based

MarketCloud would like to automatically display product suggestions on SalesCore to the salespeople trying to sell products to the customers. Suggestions would be made based on customers' information and their past interaction records with the salesperson; suggestions would therefore be customized for each customer. In other words, SalesCore is based on a recommendation engine used in a pull (inbound calls) or push (outbound calls) context. Salespeople would be able to incorporate in their sales strategy the suggested products while on a call with their customers.

To implement this idea, MarketCloud needs to build a recommendation engine and embed it into SalesCore's platform, which, from a model training and deployment standpoint, presents several challenges. We'll present these challenges in this section, and in the next section we'll show MLOps strategies that allow the company to handle each of them.

Scalability and Customizability

MarketCloud's business model (selling software for client companies to help them sell their own products) presents an interesting situation. Each client company has its own dataset, mainly about its products and customers, and it doesn't wish to share the data with other companies.

If MarketCloud has around four thousand clients using SalesCore, that means instead of having a universal recommender system for all the clients, it would need to create four thousand different systems. MarketCloud needs to come up with a way to build four thousand recommendation systems as efficiently as possible since there is no way it can handcraft that many systems one by one.

Monitoring and Retraining Strategy

Each of the four thousand recommendation engines would be trained on the customer data of the corresponding client. Therefore, each of them would be a different model, yielding a different performance result and making it nearly impossible for the company to manually keep an eye on all four thousand. For example, the recommendation engine for client A in the beverage industry might consistently give good product suggestions, while the engine for client B in the telecommunication sector might seldom provide good suggestions. MarketCloud needed to come up with a way to automate the monitoring and the subsequent model retraining strategy in case the performance degraded.

Real-Time Scoring

In many situations, MarketCloud's clients use SalesCore when they are talking to their customers on the phone. The sales negotiation evolves every single minute during the call, and the salesperson needs to adjust the strategy during the interaction with the customer, so the recommendation engine has to be responsive to real-time requests.

For example, imagine you as a salesperson are on a call with your customer to sell telecommunication devices. The customer tells you what his office looks like, the existing infrastructure at the office such as an optic fiber, the type of WiFi network, and so forth. Upon entering this information in SalesCore, you want the platform to give you a suggestion for the products that your customer could feasibly purchase. This response from the platform needs to be in real time, not 10 minutes later, after the call, or on the following day.

Ability to Turn Recommendations On and Off

Responsible AI principles acknowledge that retaining human involvement is important. This can be done through a human-in-command design,[1] by which it should be possible *not* to use the AI. In addition, adoption is likely to be low if users cannot override AI recommendations. Some clients value using their own intuition about which products to recommend to their customers. For this reason, MarketCloud wants to give its clients full control to turn the recommendation engine on and off so that the clients can use the recommendations when they want.

Pipeline Structure and Deployment Strategy

To efficiently build four thousand recommendation engines, MarketCloud decided to make one data pipeline as a prototype and duplicate it four thousand times. This prototype pipeline consists of the necessary data preprocessing steps and a single recommendation engine, built on an example dataset. The algorithms used in the recommendation engines will be the same across all four thousand pipelines, but they will be trained with the specific data associated with each client (see Figure 10-2).

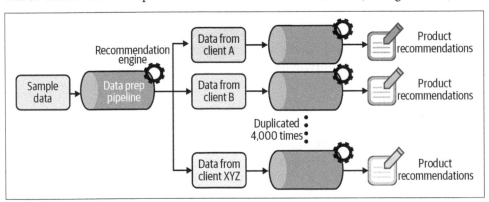

Figure 10-2. Image of data pipeline structure for MarketCloud's recommendation engine project

In this way, MarketCloud can efficiently launch four thousand recommendation systems. The users will still retain some room for customization, because the engine is trained with their own data, and each algorithm will work with different parameters —i.e., it's adopted to the customer and product information of each client.

What makes it possible to scale up a single pipeline to four thousand pipelines is the universal schema of the dataset. If a dataset from client A has 100 columns whereas

---

1 For an explanation of human-in-command design, see Karen Yeung, "Responsibility and AI" (Council of Europe study, DGI(2019)05), 64, footnote 229 (*https://oreil.ly/p5hJR*).

client B has 50, or if the column "number of purchased items" from client A is an integer whereas the same column from client B is a string, they would need to go through different preprocessing pipelines.

Although each client has different customer and product data, at the point that this data is registered on SalesCore, it acquires the same number of columns and the same data types for each column. This makes things easier, as MarketCloud simply needs to copy a single pipeline four thousand times.

Each recommendation system embedded in the four thousand pipelines will have different API endpoints. On the surface, it looks like when a user clicks the "show product recommendations" button, SalesCore displays a list of suggested products. But in the background, what is happening is that by clicking the button, the user is hitting the specific API endpoint associated with the ranked product lists for the specific customer.

Monitoring and Feedback

Maintaining four thousand recommendation systems is not an easy task, and while there have already been many MLOps considerations until this point, this is maybe the most complex part. Each system's performance needs to be monitored and updated as needed. To implement this monitoring strategy at a large scale, MarketCloud can automate the scenario for retraining and updating the models.

Retraining Models

Clients obtain new customers, some of the customers churn, every once in a while new products are added to or dropped from their catalogs; the bottom line is that customer and product data are constantly changing, and recommendation systems have to reflect the latest data. It's the only way they can maintain the quality of the recommendation, and, more importantly, avoid a situation such as recommending a WiFi router that is outdated and no longer supported.

To reflect the latest data, the team could program a scenario to automatically update the database with the newest customer and product data, retraining the model with the latest datasets every day at midnight. This automation scenario could then be implemented in all four thousand data pipelines.

The retraining frequency can differ depending on the use case. Thanks to the high degree of automation, retraining every night in this case is possible. In other contexts, retraining could be triggered by various signals (e.g., signification volume of new information or drift in customer behavior, be it aperiodic or seasonal).

In addition, the delay between the recommendation and the point in time at which its effect is evaluated has to be taken into account. If the impact is only known with a delay of several months, it is unlikely that retraining every day is adequate. Indeed, if the behavior changes so fast that retraining it every day is needed, it is likely that the model is completely outdated when it is used to make recommendations several months after the most recent ones in the training data.

Updating Models

Updating models is also one of the key features of automation strategies at scale. In this case, for each of the four thousand pipelines, retrained models must be compared to the existing models. Their performances can be compared using metrics such as RMSE (root-mean-square error), and only when the performance of the retrained model beats the prior one does the retrained model get deployed to SalesCore.

Runs Overnight, Sleeps During Daytime

Although the model is retrained every day, users do not interact directly with the model. Using the updated model, the platform actually finishes calculating the ranked list of products for all the customers during the night. On the following day, when a user hits the "show product recommendations" button, the platform simply looks at the customer ID and returns the ranked list of products for the specific customer.

To the user, it looks as if the recommendation engine is running in real time. In reality, however, everything is already prepared overnight, and the engine is sleeping during daytime. This makes it possible to get the recommendation instantly without any downtime.

Option to Manually Control Models

Although the monitoring, retraining, and updating of the models is fully automated, MarketCloud still leaves room for its clients to turn the models on and off. More precisely, MarketCloud allows the users to choose from three options to interact with the models:

- Turn on to get the recommendation based on the most updated dataset
- Freeze to stop retraining with the new data, but keep using the same model
- Turn off to completely stop using the recommendation functionality of SalesCore

Machine learning algorithms attempt to convert practical knowledge into meaningful algorithms to automate processing tasks. However, it is still good practice to leave room for users to rely on their domain knowledge, as they are presumed to be far more capable of identifying, articulating, and demonstrating day-to-day process problems in business.

The second option is important because it allows users to stay in the current quality of the recommendation without having the recommendation engines updated with the newer data. Whether the current model is replaced with a retrained one depends on the mathematical evaluation based on metrics such as the RMSE. However, if users feel that the product recommendations on SalesCore are already working well for pushing sales, they have the choice not to risk changing the recommendation quality.

Option to Automatically Control Models

For those that don't want to manually handle the models, the platform could also propose A/B testing so that the impact of new versions is tested before fully switching to them. Multi-armed bandit algorithms (an algorithm that allows for maximization of the revenue of a user facing multiple slot machines, each with a different probability to win and a different proportion of the money given back on average) are used for this purpose.

Let's assume that several model versions are available. The goal is to use the most efficient one, but to do that, the algorithm obviously has to first learn which is the most efficient. Therefore, it balances these two objectives: sometimes, it tries algorithms that may not be the most efficient to learn if they are efficient (exploration), and sometimes it uses the version that is likely to be the most efficient to maximize the revenue (exploitation). In addition, it forgets past information, as the algorithm knows the most efficient today may not be the most efficient tomorrow.

The most advanced option consists in training different models for different KPIs (click, buy, expected revenue, etc.). A method inspired from ensemble models would then allow for the solving of conflicts between models.

Monitoring Performance

When a salesperson suggests a customer buy the products recommended by Sales-Core, the interaction of the customer with the recommended products as well as whether the customer bought them or not is recorded. This record can then be used to keep track of the performance of the recommender system, overwriting the customer and product dataset with this record to feed the most updated information to the model when it is retrained.

Thanks to this ground truth recording process, dashboards showing model performance can be presented to the user, including performance comparison from A/B testing. Because the ground truth is obtained quickly, data drift monitoring is secondary. A version of the model is trained every night, but, thanks to the freeze mechanism, the user can choose the active version based on the quantitative information. It is customary to keep the human in the loop on these high-impact decisions where the performance metrics have a hard time capturing the full context around the decision.

In the case of A/B testing, it is important that only one experiment be done at a time on a group of customers; the impact of combined strategies cannot be simply added. With such considerations in mind, it is possible to build a sound baseline to perform a counterfactual analysis and derive the increased revenue and/or the decreased churn linked to a new strategy.

Apart from this, MarketCloud can also monitor the algorithm performance at a macro level, by checking how many clients froze or turned off the recommender systems. If many clients turned off the recommender systems, that's a strong indicator that they are not satisfied with the recommendation quality.

Closing Thoughts

This use case is peculiar in the sense that MarketCloud built a sales platform that many other companies use to sell products, where the ownership of the data belongs to each company, and the data cannot be shared across companies. This brings a challenging situation where MarketCloud must create different recommender systems for each of the users instead of pooling all the data to create a universal recommendation engine.

MarketCloud can overcome this obstacle by creating a single pipeline into which data from many different companies can be fed. By having the data go through an automated recommendation engine training scenario, MarketCloud created many recommendation engines trained on different datasets. Good MLOps processes are what allow the company to do this at scale.

It's worth noting that though this use case is fictionalized, it is based on reality. The real-life team that tackled a similar project took around three months to finish. The team used a data science and machine learning platform to orchestrate the duplication of a single pipeline to four thousand copies and to automate the processes to feed corresponding datasets to each pipeline and train the models. Of necessity, they accepted trade-offs between the recommendation quality and scalability to efficiently launch the product. If the team had carefully crafted a custom recommendation engine for each of the four thousand pipelines by, for example, choosing the best algorithm for each client, the recommendation engines would have been of a higher quality, but they would have never been able to complete the project with such a small team in such a short period of time.

CHAPTER 11

MLOps in Practice: Consumption Forecast

Nicolas Omont

Predictions at various times and geographical scales play an important role in the operation of a power grid. They allow for simulation of possible future states of the system and for making sure that it can safely operate. This chapter will walk through a machine learning model life cycle and MLOps use case for consumption forecasting, including business considerations, data collection, and implementation decisions. Though this particular chapter is focused on power grids, the considerations and particularities of the use case can be generalized to other industrial cases that use consumption forecasting.

Power Systems

Bulk power systems are the backbone of power grids. Also called transmission networks, they form the core of the system that keeps the lights on. These systems are mainly composed of lines and transformers, which are indirectly connected with most producers and consumers through distribution networks that take care of the last few kilometers of transmission. As illustrated in Figure 11-1, only the largest producers and consumers are directly connected to the bulk system.

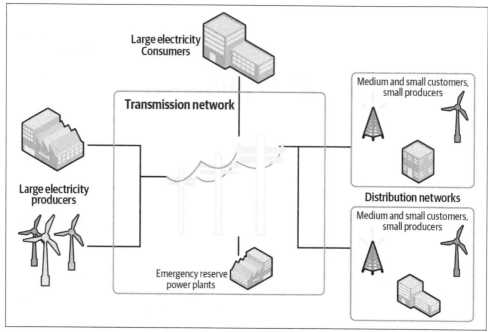

Figure 11-1. A sample bulk power system, to which only the largest producers and consumers are directly connected

The longer the transmission distance and the larger the energy volume to be transmitted, the higher the voltage used: on the lower end, a few tens of kilovolts for a few tens of megawatts over a few tens of kilometers; on the upper end, one million volts for a few thousand megawatts over a few thousand kilometers. (A line with a capacity of one megawatt can be used to provide power to around one thousand inhabitants in Europe.) The operation of transmission systems has always required a lot of communications and computations because of its properties:

No energy storage

The network stores a meaningless amount of energy—less than one second of consumption in the grid and up to 30 seconds in the alternators and motors. By way of contrast, a gas network stores several hours of consumption in its pipeline. Therefore, actions have to be taken very quickly to balance production and consumption and avoid blackouts.

Weak flow control

On telecommunication networks, congestions are handled by dropping packets or by not establishing a call. There is no equivalent mechanism in power grids, which means the power flow on a grid element can be higher than its operating limit. Actions have to be taken after a few seconds to a few hours of overload depending on the technology and the severity. Flow control technologies do exist, but there is a trade-off between flow control and instantaneous balance: the power has to find a path from generation to consumption.

Because of these two properties, the grid operator always has to anticipate the contingencies: if this grid element fails, will the overload on the remaining elements remain acceptable? The anticipation is done on several timescales, from the next five minutes to the next five decades. The actions to be taken depend on the horizon. For example:

- Below five minutes: no human action is possible. Automatic actions should already be well defined.

- Between five minutes and a few hours ahead: production schedule and grid topology adaptation (opening of breakers and other flow control technologies).

- A few days ahead: maintenance schedule adaptations.

- A few seasons ahead: maintenance schedule adaptations, contracts with producers or consumers to guarantee power capacity or limit power generation or consumption.

- From 5 to 50 years ahead: investment in grid elements. Lines and transformers have standard life expectancies of several decades; practically, it is expected that some grid elements will last over one hundred years.

Another concern is anticipating at different geographical scales. While some contingencies only have effects on a small part of the grid, some may have a continental impact and may require coordinated actions among several countries to mitigate their effects. As a result, operating the grid requires:

1. Collecting data over a wide geographical area with strong time constraints.

2. Processing data to anticipate and act accordingly.

Data Collection

Collecting past data is the first step to making forecasts. There are two largely independent sources of data: the SCADA (supervisory control and data acquisition) system and the metering system. Depending on the prediction use case, one or the other may be used.

The SCADA system collects data in real time to provide an up-to-date view of the system to the operator. It also allows commands to be sent to network equipment— for example to open and close a breaker. The most impressive representation of the system is the synoptic screen found in most control rooms as shown in Figure 11-2.

Figure 11-2. The SCADA system typically refreshes thousands of measurements about flows, consumption, and generation on the grid every 10 seconds or less

Some measurements are intentionally redundant, such as measuring power loss. If the power flow is measured at each end of a line, then the difference between them is equal to the losses on the line. These losses can be physically estimated so that it is possible to handle the case when one measure is missing, to detect anomalies, or to improve the precision of the estimates.

The process that uses this redundancy to produce a state of the network is called the state estimation, and it is run every few minutes. When an operating limit is not satisfied, the SCADA system raises an alarm. However, the SCADA cannot raise an alarm when an operating limit would not be satisfied if one of the grid elements went out of order.

Simulations of network element loss (N-1 simulation) on the consistent state produced by the state estimation are run on a regular basis, and the value of SCADA data fades quickly; therefore, when it is historized, it is not consolidated; missing values are usually not input, and anomalies are usually not corrected. State estimations are used by a variety of processes so that they are usually historized over a few months to a few years.

The metering system that is used for invoicing does not need to be as reactive as the SCADA system, but should be precise. It focuses on generation and consumption, not flow. Rather than monitoring instantaneous power, it records the withdrawn or injected energy over a period of time that ranges between a few minutes and one hour.

The information it gathers was previously made available after a delay of a day or more. Newer systems make it available within a few minutes. However, consolidation and validation are usually needed when there are missing measurements or anomalies so that the final data is still usually available within a few working days. This data is well historized.

Problem Definition: Machine Learning, or Not Machine Learning?

Not all use cases are appropriate for machine learning. Some can be solved more easily and cheaply in other ways. The techniques used to make forecasts for the type of use case presented here are different in these three situations as shown in Table 11-1.

Table 11-1. Forecasting techniques by use case

Use case	Forecasting technique
The forecast uncertainty comes from a part of the system that the operator cannot change.	Changing the weather is, practically speaking, impossible. As a result, wind and photovoltaic (PV) generation, as well as heating and air conditioning, can safely be considered exogenous. This makes them good candidates for direct machine learning forecasting. These forecasts can leverage meteorological forecasts or climatic scenarios, depending on the horizon. Meteorological forecasts are available only a few days ahead, though some models now predict trends over a few months.
The forecast uncertainty comes from a part of the system that the operator can somehow influence.	For example, strictly speaking, the consumption should not be forecasted, but rather the demand. The difference between consumption and demand is that the consumption is somehow at the hand of the operator that can choose not to serve the demand by switching off the consumers. For the same reason, the photovoltaic and wind production potential is forecasted, not the actual production.
The forecast uncertainty comes from a part of the system that some other actors can control and anticipate.	For example, for dispatchable power units where the operator can switch them on or off, it is better to ask for the schedules from the operator. If this is not possible, it may be better to reproduce the way the schedules are made—for instance, the operator may start the plant if the power price is higher than the plant fuel cost. In such cases, the forecasts may rely on techniques like agent-based modeling. Large factories are likely to have consumption schedules based on their operational production schedules. Distribution grid topology is also likely to be scheduled ahead of time, as maintenance operations require advanced planning. In all these cases, it is often better to ask for the schedules than to use machine learning to forecast them.

Spatial and Temporal Resolution

Due to the law of large numbers, the forecast uncertainty decreases when the consumption is spatially or temporally aggregated. While it is hard to forecast the hourly consumption of an individual household because people are not machines, it is surprisingly easy for populations of a few million, and is relatively easy to forecast the monthly consumption of such a population as well.

As a result, a forecast system is often hierarchical, with several levels of forecasts that are linked together by constraints. That is, regional forecasts should sum up to the country-wide forecasts, and hourly forecasts should sum up to the daily forecast.

Let's take a striking example to illustrate this. Electric traction trains have a worrying consumption pattern for grid operators because they move, with a typical train line being fed by a different substation every 10 to 50 kilometers. As a result, the operator sees consumption of a few megawatts switching from substation to substation every 10 minutes or so. It creates several issues:

- The forecast is relatively easy at the line level because the train is always consuming somewhere and because trains usually circulate at fixed hours. As a result, a machine learning approach is likely to work.

- The forecast of the energy withdrawn over a long period at a given substation is also relatively easy, because the train will go through the corresponding part of the line.

- But because the operator wants to know if the train will create an overload when circulating, a consistent set of forecasts is needed:
  — The train should withdraw power at one location at a time only.
  — Each substation should see a consumption spike at some point in time so that a fine-grained time resolution is needed.

As a result, the solution depends on the goal of the prediction:

- On a day-to-day basis, an average solution that splits the train consumption over all substations is not acceptable, as potential overloads may be missed. A worst-case solution that assigns the train consumption to all substations may be more acceptable, though it will anticipate spurious overloads as the overall consumption will be too large.

- However, to schedule the maintenance of one of the lines that feeds the region, the exact location of the consumption is likely to have no impact as long as it is not counted several times.

When designing the forecast system, trade-offs will have to be made, as the perfect system is unlikely to exist. If the system has a lot of margin, few or no overloads are expected so that the forecasting system can be coarse. However, if the grid is operated close to its limits, the system has to be carefully crafted.

Implementation

Once data is collected, either by the SCADA system or by the metering system, it has to be historized. In addition to storing the raw data, some processing is required:

- Temporal aggregations, for example over a five-minute period: Either the average value or a high quantile value is kept. The average is representative of the energy consumed over the period, and the high quantile is useful to assess if constraints occurred.

- Disaggregations: When only the withdrawal is measured, the production and the consumption have to be separately estimated. Usually, consumption is what remains after removing the best possible estimation of distributed generation (wind, PV, etc.). Machine learning can be useful to perform these estimations.

- Spatial aggregations: As the system is balanced, it is possible to compute the consumption of a region by computing the difference between the local production and the exchanges with the neighboring regions. This was historically very useful because the production was easy to monitor because there were only a few very large generation units and a few lines with neighboring countries. Nowadays, it tends to be more complex as distributed generation is more widespread.

- Missing value imputation: A measurement may be missing. In the SCADA system, rules exist to replace a missing value with an older or a typical value in real time. In the metering system, the imputation is a heavy impact process as it will be reflected directly on the customer's invoice.

Data is then stored in different databases. Data used in short-term critical processes is stored in high-availability systems in which redundancy allows rapid recovery from the loss of a data center. Data used in longer-term processes (invoicing, reports, ML model training) is stored in ordinary IT databases. Overall, the number of monitored grid elements will range between 1,000 and 100,000. This means that they generate a reasonable volume of data by today's standards. Scalability is not such an issue either, as bulk power grids do not grow anymore in developed countries.

Modeling

Once the data preparation has been finished, the data scientist typically has access to a few hundred time series of production and consumption at various withdrawal points of the grid. They have to develop methods to predict some of them at various horizons. Their focus is usually on wind, PV, and sometimes run-of-the river hydro-electricity production potential and on demand. While wind and PV mainly depend on meteorological factors, the demand is mainly driven by economic activity, but part of it is also dependent on meteorology (for example heating and cooling).

Depending on the horizon, the modeling might look very different:

- Short-term: Up to a few days ahead, the last known values are very important to make predictions. In addition, for the same reasons, meteorological forecasts are available. Therefore, methods will leverage this information. In this case, deterministic forecasts make sense.

- Mid-term: Between a few days and a few years, the meteorology is not known, but the climate is. Statistical extrapolation of past year tendencies make sense, except if an economic crisis occurs. As a result, it is possible to draw scenarios to obtain statistical indicators (mean, confidence intervals, quantiles, etc.) about the future consumptions.

- Long-term: Investment decisions require forecasts over several decades. On this horizon, statistical extrapolations of the current trend are not enough, neither on the socio-economic side nor on the climatic side given global warming. As a result, statistical approaches have to be completed with bottom-up usage-based approaches and expert-made diversified scenarios about the future.

ML and MLOps mainly concern short-term and mid-term forecasts. Of the two, in this case, mid-term models are easier to start with: given a few years of data, the goal is to predict consumption based on:

- The calendar, with a superposition of daily, weekly, and annual cycles. Bank holidays and school vacations also have a big impact, in addition to daylight saving time.

- The meteorological variables (temperature, wind, sun). As buildings have very large thermal inertia, at least two days and up to three weeks of past temperatures may be needed.

While any kind of ML algorithm can be used, the smoothness of the predicted curve is important because the predictions are not used individually, but as daily, weekly, or annual scenarios. Many algorithms do not consider smoothness in their metrics because they rely on the hypothesis that the data is independent and identically distributed, which in our case is incorrect, since the consumption of a given day is usually correlated with the one of the previous day and the one of the previous week.

Generalized additive models (GAM) are often a good starting point: they are based on splines, so that the smoothness is guaranteed. In fact, consumption forecasting was one of the use cases for which they were developed. Combined with climatic scenarios, the ML model is then able to yield yearly consumption scenarios.

Short-term forecasts are more complex. The simplest way to proceed is to remove the mid-term forecast from the recent historical data and use standard time series techniques, such as ARIMA (autoregressive integrated moving average) or exponential smoothing, on the residuals. This allows the generation of forecasts over several days. An integrated short-term model trained on several years of data has potential advantages over this simple approach.

For example, the mid-term model is trained on realized meteorological data and not on meteorological forecasts. As a result, it gives too much importance to meteorological forecasts even though they may be wrong. A short-term model trained on meteorological forecasts would address this issue. However, although new algorithms, such as long short-term memory (LSTM) neural networks, are promising, it is hard to find a method that allows for forecasting at any time of the day for several time horizons at once in a consistent way.

When the resolution is such that the stochasticity is too large to make meaningful predictions, it is better to aggregate time series spatially or temporally and then use non-ML heuristics to split the aggregated forecasts:

- A sharing key based on past observations in the case of spatial aggregation
- An average profile based on past observations in the case of temporal aggregation

Because the grid is under constant evolution, it is likely that new injections and withdrawals appear for which no historical data is available and that ruptures occur in consumption patterns, so that past data is not relevant anymore. The forecast method has to take into account these edge cases. Ruptures could be spotted using anomaly detection methods. As soon as a rupture is identified, a simplified model could be used for as long as necessary until enough historical data is available.

Once again, neural networks could become an appealing alternative with the promise that only one model could be trained for all the consumptions instead of one model per consumption with standard methods. Indeed, with only one model, the forecast of a consumption with shallow historical data would be possible provided that its pattern looks similar to an existing pattern.

Deployment

Nowadays, the models are likely to be prototyped by a data scientist in R, Python, or MATLAB scripts. The prototype is able to prepare the data, train the model on one dataset, and score it on another. The operationalization could follow several paths:

- The prototype is fully rewritten. This is costly and not flexible but may be necessary if embedding in an operational technology (OT) system is needed.
- Only the data preparation and the scoring are rewritten, which allows for training on a different schedule. It makes sense if the training occurs once a year or so because it is good practice to regularly perform a model review to ensure that it works well and that the skills to maintain it are in place.

- Data science and machine learning platforms can be used to operationalize the prototype. These platforms are flexible and allow the transfer of prototypes to production environments in which security and scalability are guaranteed. Most consumption forecast models will be run periodically in batch mode. For more specific use cases, these platforms are able to export trained models as JAR files, SQL, PMML, PFA, and ONNX so that they can be flexibly integrated into any kind of application.

Monitoring

This section mainly discusses short-term forecasts. Indeed, mid-term and long-term forecasts are systematically impacted by drift, as the past never looks like the future, so they are almost systematically trained again before being used to make predictions. For short-term forecasts, besides IT monitoring to raise alarms if forecasts are not produced on time and warnings for events that may result in missing deadlines, the models themselves should be monitored.

The first kind of monitoring is drift monitoring. For electricity consumption, it is critical that drift monitoring is deployed together with the model. Anomaly detection and rupture detection allow teams to make sure that the trained model can be used. If not, fallback models based on shallow historical data or normative disaggregation of multiple consumption forecasts should be used. This first layer will detect drastic drifts online.

Though the data scientist will try to design models that are adaptive to the consumption level (like ARIMA), it can be useful to detect that some consumption levels are higher or lower than in the training period. This may have happened slowly, so that it was not detected online. The offline analysis of the forecasts, for example once a month if the forecasts are computed every day for the next day, offers the possibility to detect these slow drifts. In these cases, if no additional ground truth is available, it would make sense to shift to a fallback model for these consumptions.

Lastly, after the operations, it is possible to assess the performance of the prediction through various metrics like mean absolute percentage error (MAPE). If a performance drop is detected during a significant amount of time (for example, one month), retraining the corresponding models is an option as new data is available, and the retrained models may increase performance.

This requires a tight integration of the design and the production environment with CI/CD processes (as discussed at length in Chapter 6). If it is possible to handle manually the deployment of new models once a year, it is usually too costly to do so once a month. With an advanced data science and machine learning platform, it is also possible to perform shadow scoring with the new model for a few days before using it for the forecasts.

Closing Thoughts

In this chapter, we have seen how to make the data speak to assist the operation of a transmission power grid. Various ML and non-ML techniques can be used to provide forecasts for up to thousands of consumptions on timescales ranging from minutes to decades.

Thanks to MLOps, design, deployment, and monitoring processes have been standardized across several industries, and data science and machine learning platforms have been developed to support this process. Designers of consumption forecast systems can leverage these standard processes and platforms to improve the efficiency of these systems from the cost, quality, or time to value perspective.

Taking a larger step back, it's clear that different industries have a wide range of machine learning use cases, all of which have their own intricacies when it comes to defining the problem, building models, pushing to production—everything we've covered in this book. But no matter what the industry or use case, MLOps processes are consistently the thread that allows data teams (and more widely, entire organizations) to scale their machine learning efforts.

Index

A

A/B testing
  canary releases, 79
  considerations in MLOps context, 102
  of new and existing model versions, 33
  performance monitoring for marketing recommendation engine, 144
  for recommendation engines using collaborative filtering, 136
  using in online evaluation of models, 99, 101
accountability
  GxP guidelines focus on, 109
  in Responsible AI, 10, 112
accuracy, precision, and recall, 132
  metrics collected in preproduction model testing, 65
adversarial attacks, 68
AI, 112
  (see also Responsible AI)
  new wave of AI-specific regulations, 111-112
  Responsible AI, MLOps for, 9
AIOps versus MLOps, 3
algorithms (machine learning), 23, 44
  computing power considerations, 45
  MLOps considerations by algorithm type, 45
  online learning, 88
  requirement for tabular input data, 47
  smoothness of predicted curve, 154
analytics use cases, understanding and classifying, 118
anomaly detection, 71

anonymizing or pseudo-anonymizing data, 36
Apache Spark, 78
APIs
  marketing recommendation engine API endpoints, 142
  REST API for model-as-a-service or live-scoring model, 28
ARIMA (autoregressive integrated moving average), 154, 156
artifacts (ML), 75-76
assumptions (model), 57
auditability, 112, 116
  aiding with QA for machine learning, 67
  and reproducibility, 67
automation
  automated feature selection, 48
  automated model deployment, 29
  automated model documentation, 27
  automated model packaging and delivery, 14, 18
  automated reporting tools on all models, 14
  automatically controlling models, marketing recommendation system, 144
  in experimentation during model development, 50
  feedback loop, 132
  of tests in testing pipeline, 76
  of versioning and reproducibility tasks, 58

B

batch scoring, 77
  volume of data becoming too large, distributing computation, 82
Bayesian tests, 34

embedded models, 28
embeddings, 48
engaging and educating groups responsible for
    governance, 123
environmental, social, and governance (ESG)
    performance indicators, 36
environments
    changing rapidly, multiplying model risks,
        70
    information needed by data scientists, 53
    providing exact description for model ver-
        sion management, 79
    reproducibility and, 58
ethical position, establishing in MLOps, 118
EU
    General Data Protection Regulation
        (GDPR), 35, 110
    key requirements for trustworthy AI appli-
        cations, 111
evaluation datasets, 44
experimentation in model development, 49-51
    impacts on MLOps strategy, 50
    marketing recommendation engines, 138
explainability, 27
    for decisions made by ML models affecting
        humans, 54
    in Responsible AI, 113
exploratory data analysis (see EDA)

F

Facebook-Cambridge Analytica affair, 106
fairness
    reassuring public that ML is fair, 106
    requirements having dimensioning con-
        straints on model development, 54
    subpopulation analysis and model fairness,
        66
feature drift, 92
feature stores, 49
features, 24
    controlling feature-value intervals, 71
    drift attributed to, use in mitigating impact
        of drift, 95
    engineering and selection, 25, 47-49
        feature engineering techniques, 47
        impacts of feature selection on MLOps
            strategy, 48
    statistical test on data from source and tar-
        get distribution, 94

federated learning approach to model retrain-
    ing, 34
feedback loop, 95-103
    automating or not, 132
    infrastructure, main components of, 96
    logging, 96
    model evaluation, 97-99
        logical model, 97
        model evaluation store, 98
    online evaluation of models in production,
        99-102
        A/B testing, 101
        champion/challenger, 100
financial crisis of 2007-2008, 109
financial model risk management regulation,
    109
financial risk management techniques, 130
Flask framework, 29
forecasting, 147
    (see also consumption forecast for power
        grid)
    forecasting techniques by use case, 151
    spatial and temporal resolution of consump-
        tion, 151

G

GAM (generalized additive models), 154
GDPR (General Data Protection Regulation),
    35, 110
generalization capacity (models), 42
Git, 75
Google, smartphone keyboard software,
    GBoard, 34
governance, 34-38, 105-125
    AI-specific regulations, new wave of,
        111-112
        status of AI governance initiatives
            worldwide, 111
    application to MLOps, 36
        data governance, 36
        process governance, 37
    critical role in machine learning security, 69
    current regulations driving MLOps gover-
        nance, 108-111
        financial model risk management, 109
        GDPR and CCPA data privacy regula-
            tions, 110
        pharmaceutical regulation in US, GxP,
            109

decoupled ground truth and prediction, 90
examples of model prediction and generalization, 43
ground truth for model predictions, 31
input drift and, 31
probabilities
distances between probability distributions,
measuring, 132
produced by models used for risk assessment, 131
problem definition and data acquisition, com-
sumer credit risk management MLOps
application, 130
problem definition, using machine learning or
not, 151-152
process governance, 37
effective implementation, difficulties of, 37
production, deploying to, 73-84
building ML artifacts, 75-76
using testing pipeline on model, 75
CI/CD pipelines, 73
consumer credit risk management model,
132
consumption forecast prototype models,
155
containerization, 79-81
deployment strategies, 77-79
categories of model deployment, 77
considerations in sending models to production, 78
maintenance of models in production,
79
scaling deployments, 81-83
requirements and challenges, 83
production, preparing for, 59-72
consumer credit risk management model,
131
key ideas, summary of, 72
machine learning security, 67-69
model risk evaluation, 63-64
model risk mitigation, 69-72
changing environments, 70
interactions between models, 70
model misbehavior, 71
quality assurance for machine learning,
64-66
reproducibility and auditability for models,
66
runtime environments, 60-63

adaptation from development to production environments, 60-62
data access before validation and launch
to poduction, 62
final thoughts on, 62
productionalization and deploymnt of models,
27-29
model deployment requirements, 29
model deployment types and contents, 28
progressive or canary rollouts, 69
project criticality and operationalization
approaches to risk assessment, 107
provenance of data, 113
pruning models, 61
public opinion, influence on ML governance,
106
push or pull recommendations, 136
Python, 9, 61, 155

Q
QA (quality assurance) for machine learning,
64-66
key testing considerations, 65
providing clear view of model performance
and facilitating auditability, 67
quantization, 61

R
R language, 155
RACI (responsible, accountable, consulted,
informed), 119
randomness, 57
random sampling, 91
real-time scoring, 77
logging streaming data, 83
marketing recommendation engine model,
140
recommendation engines, 135
(see also marketing recommendation
engines)
rise of, 135-137
deciding on push or pull recommendations, 136
turning recommendations on/off, 141
red-black deployment, 78
regulations, 118
AI-specific, new wave of, 111-112
current, driving MLOps governance,
108-111

About the Authors

Mark Treveil has designed products in fields as diverse as telecommunications, banking, and online trading. His own startup led a revolution in governance in UK local government, where it still dominates. He is now part of the Dataiku Product Team based in Paris.

Nicolas Omont is VP of operations at Artelys, where he is developing mathematical optimization solutions for energy and transport. He previously held the role of Dataiku product manager for ML and advanced analytics. He holds a PhD in computer science, and he's been working in operations research and statistics for the past 15 years, mainly in the telecommunications and energy utility sectors.

Clément Stenac is a passionate software engineer, CTO, and cofounder at Dataiku. He oversees the design and development of the Dataiku DSS Enterprise AI Platform. Clément was previously head of product development at Exalead, leading the design and implementation of web-scale search engine software. He also has extensive experience with open source software, as a former developer of the VideoLAN (VLC) and Debian projects.

Kenji Lefèvre is VP of product at Dataiku. He oversees the product road map and the user experience of the Dataiku DSS Enterprise AI Platform. He holds a PhD in pure mathematics from University of Paris VII, and he directed documentary movies before switching to data science and product management.

Du Phan is a machine learning engineer at Dataiku, where he works in democratizing data science. In the past few years, he has been dealing with a variety of data problems, from geospatial analysis to deep learning. His work now focuses on different facets and challenges of MLOps.

Joachim Zentici is an engineering director at Dataiku. Joachim graduated in applied mathematics from Ecole Centrale Paris. Prior to joining Dataiku in 2014, he was a research engineer in computer vision at Siemens Molecular Imaging and Inria. He has also been a teacher and a lecturer. At Dataiku, Joachim has made multiple contributions including managing the engineers in charge of the core infrastructure, building the team for the plug-ins and ecosystem efforts, and leading the global technology training program for customer-facing engineers.

Adrien Lavoillotte is an engineering director at Dataiku where he leads the team responsible for machine learning and statistics features in the software. He studied at ECE Paris, a graduate school of engineering, and worked for several startups before joining Dataiku in 2015.

Makoto Miyazaki is a data scientist at Dataiku and responsible for delivering hands-on consulting services using Dataiku DSS for European and Japanese clients. Makoto holds a bachelor's degree in economics and a master's degree in data science, and he was also a former financial journalist with a wide range of beats, including nuclear energy and economic recoveries from the tsunami.

Lynn Heidmann received her bachelor's degree in journalism/mass communications and anthropology from the University of Wisconsin-Madison in 2008 and decided to bring her passion for research and writing into the world of tech. She spent seven years in the San Francisco Bay Area writing and running operations with Google and subsequently Niantic before moving to Paris to head content initiatives at Dataiku. In her current role, Lynn follows and writes about technological trends and developments in the world of data and AI.

Colophon

The animal on the cover of *Introducing MLOps* is an African moth called *Bunaeopsis oubie*, also known as Zaddach's Emperor, that can be found across central and eastern Africa, from Angola to Eritrea. It is a member of the *Saturniidae* family, which includes one thousand species of the world's largest moths.

This African moth has one of the largest wingspans, stretching up to 10 inches, making it bigger than some birds. Its wings have distinctive markings: one reddish brown circle on each of the four wings, dark brown stripes underneath, and white strokes bordering the thorax and along the outer edges of each wing. Moth antennae are thick and feathered. Their entire bodies repel water with a wax coating that covers their hairs and the scales on their wings.

Moths tend to be attracted to white, fragrant flowers, which they sniff out easily at night and pollinate well with their fuzzy, sticky bodies. Many animals and birds depend on moths in their diets, including owls and bats. Moth caterpillars are prey to lizards, birds, and many small mammals.

Many of the animals on O'Reilly's covers are endangered; all of them are important to the world.

The cover illustration is by Karen Montgomery, based on a black and white engraving from *Encyclopedie D'Histoire Naturelle*. The cover fonts are Gilroy Semibold and Guardian Sans. The text font is Adobe Minion Pro; the heading font is Adobe Myriad Condensed; and the code font is Dalton Maag's Ubuntu Mono.

O'REILLY®

There's much more
where this came from.

Experience books, videos, live online
training courses, and more from O'Reilly
and our 200+ partners—all in one place.

Learn more at oreilly.com/online-learning

Milton Keynes UK
Ingram Content Group UK Ltd.
UKHW032255191024
449882UK00007B/114